GOD.

Noun or Verb?

Stories of complaints about God — his response

Frank DeVries

TRAFFORD

• Canada • UK • Ireland • USA •

Note for Librarians: A cataloguing record for this book is available from Library and Archives Canada at www.collectionscanada.ca/amicus/index-e.html
ISBN 1-4120-8645-0

Printed in Victoria, BC, Canada. Printed on paper with minimum 30% recycled fibre. Trafford's print shop runs on "green energy" from solar, wind and other environmentally-friendly power sources.

TRAFFORD
PUBLISHING

Offices in Canada, USA, Ireland and UK
This book was published *on-demand* in cooperation with Trafford Publishing. On-demand publishing is a unique process and service of making a book available for retail sale to the public taking advantage of on-demand manufacturing and Internet marketing. On-demand publishing includes promotions, retail sales, manufacturing, order fulfilment, accounting and collecting royalties on behalf of the author.

Book sales for North America and international:
Trafford Publishing, 6E–2333 Government St.,
Victoria, BC v8t 4p4 CANADA
phone 250 383 6864 (toll-free 1 888 232 4444)
fax 250 383 6804; email to orders@trafford.com
Book sales in Europe:
Trafford Publishing (uk) Limited, 9 Park End Street, 2nd Floor
Oxford, UK ox1 1hh UNITED KINGDOM
phone 44 (0)1865 722 113 (local rate 0845 230 9601)
facsimile 44 (0)1865 722 868; info.uk@trafford.com
Order online at:
trafford.com/06-0401

10 9 8 7 6 5 4 3 2

In Memory of Ronald

In times of calamity, ill health, or sadness, many have raised an angry fist to the Great Unseen in the sky demanding to know, "Why me?" That question was not always asked in times of good fortune, good health, and joy...

Ed Seirv,

ACKNOWLEDGEMENTS

During the writing of the book the help of my friend the *Rev. Henk Numan*, pastor of First Christian Reformed Church in Vancouver B.C., was invaluable. His enthusiastic support together with his theological insights and eye for inaccuracies were of inestimable help to me. I am indebted to *Dr. Calvin Seerveld*, Professor Emeritus of the Institute for Christian Studies in Toronto, Ontario, who went out of his way critiquing the book. His knowledge of scripture and sensitivity to the Lord's leading caused me to make a number of changes. My life-long friend *Dr. John Van Dyk*, Professor of Education at Dordt College in Sioux Center, Iowa, with his sharp insights and storied sense of logic convinced me to rework an important section of the book.

After an early reading of the manuscript my son *Peter* wholeheartedly endorsed my effort, an affirmation that helped me see the project through to its completion. Well-known Ottawa calligraphist and graphic designer *Lance Butler*, now of Nanaimo, B.C., honored me by conceiving and planning out the cover of the book, while *Barry Conway, M.D.*, of Victoria, B.C., kindly reviewed the medical episodes, and suggested a number of changes.

However, throughout it has been my forbearing wife *Celia* who has influenced me more than anyone; she often suggested milder, more sensitive ways in which to express myself. Her frequent laughter, her singing, her wonderful sense of humor and her perceptive spirit filled my days with joy, and were sustaining forces to me.

Frank DeVries

CONTENTS

Prologue   1

Epilogue   111

GOD.
Noun or Verb?
Stories of complaints about God – his response

PROLOGUE

The World Council of Churches, established in the late 1940s in Amsterdam, is founded on principles of Christian encounter, dialogue and collaboration. Today, AD 2059, nearly all orthodox streams of Christianity have softened any previous intransigent positions, and have returned to the Council's fold. Currently, the W.C.C. comprises nearly 600 million believers from more than 150 countries.

Traditionally the World Council of Churches holds a General Assembly every seventh year, the last one having been held in 2054. Unbeknownst to this body God decided that on the occasion of their planned twentieth Assembly in 2061 he would use his servant Pieter Retief, together with the W.C.C. governing body, to deliver an important message to all people on earth. God resolved to do this because over the years and centuries many had called into question his actions in matters of sickness, accident, and various "natural" disasters. Many believers, yet oddly also many unbelievers, frequently had held him "personally" accountable for misfortunes that had befallen them.

God felt that by using the Council of Churches as an intermediary there might be a chance to foster a higher level of understanding between himself, and the people on earth. At minimum, he thought, it would promote a clearer vision of who he was, and what he was about. If successful, it would increase significantly the level of happiness and contentment of all those who had originally committed themselves to him, and might even cause unbelievers to mull over possible reasons why they might be on the planet. Strangely, even though the faithful had supposedly seen the great light, many of them, too, appeared to walk in the same darkness as those who had not.

Over the centuries God had revealed himself to humankind in each of three ways: the Bible, his son Jesus Christ, and creation. The Bible records the history of the people of Israel and their relationship to God. Detailed in it, too, are the birth, death and resurrection of Jesus. Moreover, in and through the creation he had made himself known to all: from the whirling vastness of the cosmos to sub-atomic particles, from spider silk and baleen whales to the crystalline structures of molybdenum and snow-flakes, from the miracle of the cotyledon to that of metamorphosis.

By rights this three-pronged revelation should have resulted in a massive love-in for the creator of all. The history of God's people, together with the story of a crucified and risen Savior, should have functioned as the glasses through which the true nature of creation could be seen, heard and felt. But rather than worship of the creator, many had become intoxicated with the beauty of nature, and had begun worshiping it instead. This had made God sad.

However, to deliver his message and communicate meaningfully with his people, God first had to initiate a new way to do this. He had to establish an unequivocally verifiable system of communication. Of old, communication between God and his people had usually taken the form of prayer. However, claimed results of prayer had always been subjective, hence unverifiable, and forever open to personal interpretation. This time prayer simply would not do. So now, as e-mail as well as Instant Messaging had gone the way of the Homing Pigeon, God decided to work within the current human system of communication, and use Imanto.

Imanto was the result of a synthesis of Instant Messaging and a recently revised and updated version of Ido, the artificial international language and flourishing offspring of Esperanto. The combination had worked well. Imanto used a computer keyboard that utilized either singly or in combination 212 letters, numbers, characters and symbols. With the help of Satellite Laser (which by now had become the bane of law enforcement agencies world-wide) computer communication on the planet had taken off as never before. In a nanosecond any message could be sent to anyone anywhere on the planet or to the eleven colonies on Luna and Mars.

Furthermore, because of instant electronic translation into any language and most dialects, communication was no longer bound by language constraints. Any language could be understood immediately by anyone who could read. However, complicating matters, and of increasing concern to many, was "Moore's law." This law pointed out that computer microchips were being replaced at ever increasing speeds, and so it was predicted that before long the effects of "Moore's law" would begin to imperil even the current Imanto intercommunications system. Not that Imanto in any significant way had promoted better understanding between people . . . .

Terms like "nanotechnology" and "extreme ultraviolet lithography" bore witness to an incredible speeding up of the computer age. V.N.S., Vaginal Nerve Stimulation to make people "feel happy," was the latest rage, and scientists were experimenting with computer displays optionally implanted in the human eye, devices that doubled as video cameras. Neuro-marketing geared to the subconscious desires of consumers was everywhere, the new science dealing with prosthetics for the brain was rapidly becoming an investment haven, and the benefits of direct broadband neural pathways between brain and computer occupied discussions in the board rooms of the nations.

Already technophiles called "trans-humanists" were beginning to talk about the legal rights of computers in the future and what exactly constituted being human. Once again ethics and philosophy were struggling hard to keep pace with a developing technology, and with countless people maintaining video blogs on the web, it all was beginning to surpass even the wildest prophesies of futurist William Gibson, the new Jules Vern.

CHAPTER 1

Pieter Retief

Crouched on one knee Pieter was hand-feeding the Koi. With his other hand he had slapped against one of the pieces of slate along the side of the pond, and like surfacing submarines the large fish had excitedly swum up to him, broad backs swishing away the water hyacinths and water lettuce that covered large areas of the surface. The wide-open, hungry mouths of the large carp took the specially formulated food pellets right out of his hand, making loud snorting and slurping noises as they fed.

Pieter cherished the feeling of their wet mouths in his hand. As often before, he quietly chuckled at the sounds they made. They reminded him of when his grandpa had still been alive and would greedily slurp down grandma's widely acclaimed clam chowder. He got up, reached into the small food bucket, and flung a final handful of food pellets farther away into the pond. Slowly walking back to the patio, as always wary of possible salmonella poisoning after having touched his fish, or even the pond water, he thoroughly washed his hands with soap under the outside water tap.

Pieter Retief had dozed on his lounge chair in the open porch of his home, halfway up Table Mountain on the North end of Cape Town. It had been particularly hot and humid today. The aroma of the bougainvillea that grew profusely over the partly trellised veranda lay heavy in the air. A large *Buddleja davidii*, the imported "Butterfly Bush" beside the patio belied its name, and

5

showed no butterflies whatsoever. Instead it was alive with the drone of hundreds of bees toking up on pollen.

He leaned his head back and overlooked the varied flora of his peaceful botanical paradise. Designed by his wife and himself it was anchored by the Koi pond which, stocked with Kohaku and Tashio Sanke Koi, had become the focal point of the extensive garden. But the warmth of the day together with the anesthetic drone of the bees once again began to take its toll on Dr. Retief. His eyelids became heavy, and closing his eyes, he dozed.

Recognized for his creative genius, for many years Retief had been in charge of the robotics and computer program at the advanced design department of S.A.T., South Africa Tech. However, the position had been immensely stressful, and because of that one day everything had changed for him. During a regular workday he had to be rushed to Groote Schuur hospital emergency, was diagnosed with "unstable angina," and had to spend five days in a hospital bed being tested and scanned. Though by medical definition it had not been "The Big One," it certainly had been a powerful warning. Pieter Retief wasn't stupid. At age forty-four, financially secure, he relinquished his position at S.A.T.

Seven months later his life changed again. An avid reader, he had worked himself through a book that dealt with matters far weightier than the new technology with which he had been involved for so long. He had been reading a book that up till now had sat dusty and neglected between the many other weighty tomes in his bookcase: the recently completed New Millennium version of the Bible.

As he sat in his study one time waiting for his copier to finish printing a long article, his eye had fallen on the book. Absentmindedly he had picked it up and had begun to read, in a strange way an experience not unlike that of St. Augustine. After all, it had been he who some sixteen centuries earlier had been sitting in his garden looking at a Bible, when reputedly he heard a little girl next door sing a children's song called *tolle, lege,* or, "pick it up, and read it."

As it had been for St. Augustine and untold zillions after him, for Pieter Retief the reading of Holy Writ became a life-changing experience. Several months later he received what he determined was a call from the Lord to become one of his special servants. Shortly after he once again enrolled in university, this time signing up for studies in the theology department of the Christ the King College. Four years later, at the age of forty-nine, he successfully defended his dissertation, and received his doctorate in theology *summa cum laude.*

Soon he became recognized internationally as a man of uncommon Christian insight, and within a few years the brilliantly creative electronic expert turned theologian accepted a position working full--time for the World Council of Churches. Serving at first as its head representative in the Republic of South Africa, after three successful years he was appointed as General Secretary for the entire African continent. Although he still dealt with pressures they were of an entirely different nature now, and never became problematic. God's Spirit had given him the deep satisfaction to know what life was really about: life was about *Life.*

Through times spent in prayer and meditation Pieter Retief had become acquainted with the various readily available pathways leading to peaceful solutions for the pressures of life. Preeminent among these was to experience and savor regularly God's creation: to "stop and smell the roses." He had learned the hard way how crucial, how vital this was to help relieve daily stresses. And so, once again today, he had been resting on the porch to look at his Koi, and to doze.

The construction of the pond had taken well over a year. He had not given in to the initial temptation to install more readily available and economical faux rocks for the waterfall, but had a truckload of several actual large rocks and boulders brought in and artistically stacked along the far end of the pond. A submersed pump continuously forced water over them in an irregular pattern of silvery cascading ripples and waves. The flat pieces of slate around the pond, together with the three-sectioned Japanese bridge across it, afforded him a close look at his fish anytime he so desired.

Slowly Pieter Retief opened his eyes again. The heat had not abated, and the bees were still busily buzzing in the butterfly bush. From where he lay he could see the carp as they slowly moved through the water, occasionally breaking the surface in brief flashes of red, white and black. Off and on they nipped away at some of the food pellets that still floated on the surface. Although he had had the Koi for nearly twelve years they still looked and acted vigorous and healthy. No doubt, he thought, this was partially due to the expensive biological filtration/circulation system and spa skimmer he had installed. It had been worth doing. And so Pieter Retief should have been happy. Not that he was really *un*happy, but he was tired, and certainly not overjoyed.

"Necrotizing enterocolitis" had been the diagnosis, and during the surgery it had been found the section of the colon that remained had been too diseased to be reconnected to the proximal intestine. It had to be removed: Pieter Retief's colostomy was thought to be permanent. He sighed, and looked at the carp. Blissfully unaware of their keeper's state of mind the fish swam on, dignified, and serene. But Pieter got up, and walked to his office to take the final step in an important decision he had made several days earlier: he was going to resign his position with the W.C.C.

Three days ago, without giving them a specific reason, he had informed both his wife and his close theologian friend Klaas Blik of his resolve. With no explanation given for his rather sudden decision both his wife and the good Dr. Blik had tried hard to dissuade him from it, but to no avail. It became clear that Pieter's mind was made up, and after a time both Mrs. Retief and Dr. Blik gave up flogging what now appeared to be a truly dead horse. What's more, after some further discussion, pending the endorsement from head office, Dr. Blik consented to act as his replacement in the W.C.C.

Today Pieter had made it final and had sent a videogram to his eight W.C.C. colleagues. In it he submitted his resignation, effective immediately. Still not giving any reasons for his action he informed them he no longer would either physically or by video conference attend any meetings, and asked to accept with all possible regard his friend Dr. Klaas Blik as his replacement. When finished he went back to the patio.

Unlike many who blamed God for their infirmities and discomforts, Pieter knew that Jesus himself was distraught about his condition, too. God didn't want him to be sick: the popular "Blame-It-On-God" game was not in Dr. Retief's make-up. He knew that his God was a God of Love who did not want his children to hurt, or to experience pain. Back in hospital when he had discussed this with fellow patients most would disagree with him. "If there is a God who loves us," they would argue, "Why would he let us suffer like this?" and "Why would a loving God do this to me?" they would ask, or even suggest ignominiously, "Perhaps your God is asleep? Or maybe he is dead?" And they would snicker.

Pieter leaned back. As a theologian he had faced these types of questions many times before, especially from his students. Still, when in hospital, such ill-considered questions and comments caused him more disquiet than usual, and because of it a plan had begun to take shape in his mind, a plan that with today's official resignation from the W.C.C. could be put into play. Slowly he got up and walked to his study, where in a space of about four by six meters several computers and assorted electronic contrivances vied for space with heavily laden bookcases and stacks of magazines. With some effort a weary Dr. Retief sat down. Yet in spite of his physical discomfort, his face displayed a grin not unlike that of a fully contented Cheshire cat...

CHAPTER 2

Dmitri Karamios

I t was 2059, May 5, some two years before the W.C.C. General Assembly. Dmitri Karamios, the seventy-eight year old Grand Prelate of the Russian Orthodox Church, stood by the *iconostasis*, the icon-decorated screen that separated the sanctuary from the nave. As with other screens like it, the art work on it was designed to aid the congregation in worship, to enable them to read the lessons pictorially. In an attempt to cut visually through the haze of wavering candle lights and clouds of incense, lines were strong, and colors intense. Normally the beautifully painted icons pleased the bishop's eyes, but today nothing of the sort happened.

Of late a strong feeling of alienation, of being far removed from the cares and concerns of his congregation, had taken hold of the aging bishop. Today this feeling had become even stronger. In fact, after what had happened earlier he contemplated how that very screen now not only physically, but also symbolically attested to the division that rightly or wrongly existed twixt clergy and laity. For towards the end of today's procession, during the divine liturgy of St. John Chrystosom, he had stumbled. As he had grasped the side of a pew to prevent himself from falling he had momentarily looked into the eyes of an older woman, a woman of about his own age.

He hadn't known her, though what he had seen in her eyes had disturbed him greatly, for she had looked at him with an utterly blank expression, a look of great emotional distance. He was startled by it. Who was she? He did not recognize her, and to his knowledge had never seen her before. But as he had looked around for a familiar face he was distressed to see that all the other countenances in the congregation bore the same empty, almost cold expression. Was this his congregation? Were these his parishioners? Were all these people *God's* people? Did he know *any* of them?

Staring at the *iconostasis* he again felt that strong sense of estrangement, a sense of being outside of his congregation. The memory of it made him dizzy with sudden apprehension, and with faltering steps he made his way to his office, the door to it a narrow opening in the wall to the right of the altar. After he had entered his private little domain he sat down in his old leather chair, leaned back, and took several long pulls from a bottle on the floor beside him.

After a while he got up and went to his computer desk. He leaned his arms on his knees, closed his eyes, and rested his head against the monitor. Bishop Karamios sat like that for many minutes, almost asleep. After some time he slowly sat up straight and booted the computer; he had been told he would reduce by about half the possibility of viruses if he shut it off at night. As he had never yet experienced any difficulty with computer viruses it seemed to have been a good decision.

He opened his Imanto inbox, and froze. He stared at the screen. A window had popped up that read, centered in a cursive font,

Dmitri,
Do you love me?
God.

Angrily he wondered what hacker could have put that on. And how. Had someone been in his office?

Still annoyed he picked up his worn Bible and turned to the book of Psalms. His mind kept wandering off. Pictures of the expressionless faces in his congregation together with the words of the strange question on the monitor occupied his mind, and took their toll on his concentration. With a sigh he closed his Bible, laid it in his lap, and glanced out the small window. It was an early summer night, but there was a chill in the air, a chill that seemed to find its way into his heart, bringing with it a clear sense of unease and foreboding.

As he reflected on the strange message he recalled that Jesus had posed that very same question as many as three times to Simon Peter. Who would send him such a message? And why? Determined, somewhat angrily, he went back to the computer, pressed the reply-to-sender key, and with two gnarled old index fingers slowly typed,

> It is not good to make fun of an old man.
> Remember '*AXIOS*.'
> Dmitri Karamios

He sent the message, shut off the computer, and locked the door to his office. This time he made extra sure it was locked. As he left the church he closed the heavy double doors and walked the short distance to his *dom*. Once there he undressed and, standing tall in the kind of long underwear he wore throughout the year, poured himself several ounces of vodka, tipped his head, tossed the drink, and crawled in bed. In minutes Bishop Karamios was fast asleep.

CHAPTER 3

Could this be God?

B ishop Karamios, who was also the General Secretary of the W.C.C. Conference of Churches in Europe, at this time did not yet know that a similar message had been received by the General Secretaries of all the other districts that made up the Council. However, when he used the voice-activated auto dialer to call his colleague in the Middle East on an unrelated matter, he learned that he himself had been about to be contacted by him.

It was through this Middle Eastern colleague that he learned all W.C.C. representatives of the Conferences of Churches in Asia, the Pacific, the Caribbean and Africa, as well as those of the Church Councils of Latin America, the U.S and Canada, had received the same personally addressed message, in the same cursively printed Imanto, and had been asked the same troubling question. All were puzzled, with several being quite disturbed, even angry about it. They each had struggled unsuccessfully to come to grips with the meaning and implication of the odd communication. It had been so disturbing to so many that everyone felt a videophone conference about the matter was imperative, and should be held as soon as possible.

And so it happened that a conference meeting of all the Secretaries, with the exception of one, was arranged for later that day. The Secretary not participating was the representative from Africa, Pieter Retief. However, a quick on-the-spot vote was held, and the recommended replacement in the person of Dr. Blik was accepted on an interim basis, with a final vote about a permanent appointment to be held sometime in the future.

The video conference lasted for well over two hours, but a consensus of how to deal with what was now referred to somewhat amusingly as "God's question," remained elusive. In the end it was agreed to have a follow-up conference a week later. The date was set, and all retreated to the stillness of their hearts, puzzled, confused, and vaguely uneasy. What did it all mean? Who had really sent the message? Why was it that all General Secretaries were asked the same question? Did the questioner, whoever she or he was really doubt that the W.C.C. representatives loved God? What could be the reason for the questioner to ask that question? Was it a joke, or could it really be God himself? Although the latter seemed rather unlikely, the thought did not go away entirely.

That night Karamios did not sleep well and, as he learned later, neither did any of his ecclesiastical colleagues.

CHAPTER 4

God's Message

At the second conference it was learned no one had received any additional communications. Although various suggestions were put forward, not one of the delegates knew for certain who really had posed "The Question." Hence it was pretty startling that just when the General Secretary from the Pacific region was about to make the motion to adjourn and close out, in all sectors the Secretaries' personal video screens suddenly showed two words in the same script that was used before. Startled, they all read on their personal 3-dimensional screens the question,

Well?
God

There was an immediate, stunned silence. Then the regular video picture came on again, and superficially everything seemed as moments before. This time, in a composite, all video screen monitors showed the nine representatives as usual neatly arrayed in three rows of three. And each face showed fright, and disbelief. What was going on? Who was doing this?

Everyone began to speak at once, and for some time great confusion held sway. Finally Maria Sanchez from the Latin American division, the only female delegate and current chair, broke through the discussion with a firm, "Well, folks, this is getting us nowhere. Let us take turns in giving our reaction to what just has

15

happened, and let us follow that up with your suggestions what to do next."

The proposal met with general approval. The Middle Eastern delegate put the suggestion into a motion, it was seconded and recorded, and this time in orderly fashion a discussion began. Slowly, most of the delegates began to allow for the possibility the message was indeed from God. However, what to do next took quite a bit longer.

"Let's send a message back," said some, but "Disregard the entire matter," said another. After they weighed those as well as some other alternatives, a unanimous decision was finally reached. On behalf of them all they would send an Imanto message back to the sender. It took a long time to come to an agreement what exactly to convey in the message, and for many hours the many choices were weighed. Still, in the end a consensus was reached, and it was agreed to respond with the following:

Dear God,
you know we love you!
What would you have us do?
Your servants.

The message was sent, and almost immediately the following appeared on the screen:

Dear Children,
If you love me indeed,
over the next two years collect from all people
who attend church,
as well as from those who do not,
any and all questions, criticisms or doubts they have about me.
From these criticisms select twelve representative samples.
On May 20, during your 2061 General Assembly,
I will respond to them.
God.

They all looked at each other bewilderedly. This was crazy! Was this really God, and did he really mean this? What a strange business! Everybody began to speak, with few taking the time to listen. Finally the voice of Maria Sanchez once again cut through all the talk with a forceful, "Okay, let's stop here. We shall disconnect and get together for an 'in-the-flesh' meeting within the week. I shall inform you when and where shortly. In the meantime, do reflect on what has happened these past few days. God bless you all." Her screen went blank, followed by the blanking out of the other eight screens. The meeting was over.

CHAPTER 5

Collection Organized

I n spite of the hard-working air conditioner it was hot and humid in the room. All nine W.C.C. representatives had gathered
on one of the few occasions they physically met. Due to the emer-
gent situation with what by all now was accepted to have been an
Imanto message from God, Maria Sanchez had called this meeting in a Brasilia hotel meeting room. Different from any previous
meetings, today socializing was at a minimum. The atmosphere
was tense, and after their flights many of the jet-lagged representatives looked haggard, and tired.

Presently the meeting was called to order. A round-prayer was
called for by the chair, and slowly a semblance of peace began to
pervade the room. The prayer went on for about an hour, after
which discussions began. The agenda was a short one with but
one cryptic double-edged question: what are we going to do, and
how are we going to do it?

As everyone had points of view to discuss and ideas to mull
over, the talks went on for a long time. Still, finally, a motion was
agreed upon, seconded, and passed unanimously. In it the nine
General Secretaries committed themselves to contact all governing bodies of member denominations in their individual sectors
to inform them of the strange happenings. They, in turn, would
be requested to send out immediately missives to all pastors and
priests in member- as well as non-member churches and chapels.
Special press releases were to be given to the world media to in-

form every person on the planet about the important happenings that had occurred.

Accompanying this letter, and for distribution to all church members, adherents, and anyone else who would request them, were to be packages of questionnaires. Should anyone have a complaint or doubt about any of God's actions, non-actions, or judgments, they were asked to fill in the questionnaire and return it in the pre-stamped, self-addressed envelope that was provided for sorting and final selection.

In the letter to the governing bodies it was requested to have all pertinent information reproduced in denominational magazines and congregational bulletins, and to have it read on radio and in the telemedia. Also, from their pulpits or chancels, all pastors and priests were asked to provide any additional clarification of what God had said and was planning to do with the information he would receive. All addressees were informed that at the W.C.C. head office the complaints and criticisms were going to be collected by an especially appointed committee. Finally, all were reminded that in the end only twelve representative grievances would be chosen and brought before the Lord for his response two years hence. For all these matters, both congregational and individual prayers were devoutly solicited.

Again, the time allotment in which all this was to happen was two years, the starting date being the W.C.C. announcement. As this was the month of May in the year 2059, the final selection of complaints to be presented to God was to be ready for a response by him at the May 2061 General Assembly of the W.C.C.

A form letter was prepared, and after a number of minor changes in wording was approved. The special organizing committee was appointed and directed to set up a central place of work at head office in Geneva. To speed matters, the recording clerk of the W.C.C. was instructed to have the letters sent out immediately by videograph, to be followed by the packages of questionnaires as soon as possible. The entire process of complaints about God was officially set in motion.

The meeting ended. No specific date was set for the next get-together, by general agreement that being left to be called by the chair. The tired representatives sat back in their chairs, alone with their thoughts. And so it all began.

CHAPTER 6

Geertje

In spite of her melancholy mood, Geertje had to smile. "GEEN HONDEN POEP HIER," read the sign in higher case letters, "No dog poop here." In the alley the small hand-written notice was stapled to the wall of the hardware store. Amused, she briefly wondered if the sign was meant to be read by educated dogs, or by their owners. From the main road, winding her way between several homes, Geertje proceeded towards the dyke, the picturesque walkway parallel to the main road. Both led to "downtown" Nieuwkoop.

Crossing the narrow, high bridge over the *gracht*, the narrow body of water that lay between the dyke and village proper, she stepped onto the path. Quickly she had to move to the side as two youngsters biked by on their way to school, easily sailing around a cow that had climbed up from the field to get to the water of the gracht.

The animal, its numbered yellow ear tags shimmering in the sunlight, lowered its front legs into the muddy, reed-overgrown bank beside the path and began to drink. Geertje gingerly made her way around the back of the animal and walked on to the village, an empty backpack loosely swinging in her hand.

It was a nice walk. On the west side of the dyke were the grasslands, stretching out to a poplar-lined highway in the distance. Here and there a church tower punctuated the horizon, and *kievieten*, the European killdeer, soared over the fields, flashing back

and forth the white bands on the underside of their wings as they
slalomed through the air in search of food. In the gracht on her
right several kinds of water lilies grew, some already beginning to
show bloom, and various water fowl quietly sat on nests made in
small tufts of reedy islands. Unperturbed, they did not even look
up from their clutch as Geertje walked by.

Half an hour later she entered the large, two-storey Albert
Heijn grocery store, and did her Friday shopping. Broad beans
imported from Portugal were on sale, and she ordered a dozen
jars of them to be set aside. As she was already going to carry
home two bottles of Penfolds Retreat, her favorite chardonnay,
there was no way she could carry home the beans, too. She told
Adrie, the check-out girl, she would pick them up later by car,
and then walked past the old Hoge Huys tower to go to her usual
café for her coffee fix.

At this time of day, 9:30 in the morning, it wasn't busy yet,
and Kees joined her on the patio. Kees, the owner of the café, was
an old school friend. As they sipped away on their morning drink
they both looked up at some dozen pigeons wheeling overhead,
loudly flapping their wings in the early morning sun. Nearby by
a mourning dove announced its approval of the sunny weather
with a plaintive coo-ge-re-goo, endlessly repeated.

"So how's it going, girl?" asked Kees. Geertje didn't answer
right away. What could she say? That she felt abandoned and
picked on by God? That she had been on strong anti-depressant
medication for the past six months? That Arend, her husband,
had left her? That she hadn't seen her daughter in two years? But
Kees knew all that already anyway. "Oh, I'm okay, I guess," she
answered, but the tone of her voice gave her away. "Not so good
again, eh?" said Kees, who knew somewhat of her circumstances.
Geertje did not answer. A customer came in, ordered an *uitsmijter
rosbief*, and Kees left to prepare the quintessential Dutch breakfast
of roast beef omelet, leaving Geertje alone with her thoughts.

It had been a difficult couple of years for her, these last two.
Seven years ago, after twenty years of what she thought had been

a reasonably good marriage, Arend had left her for another woman, girl, actually. She had been thirteen years younger than he and, according to Geertje's thinking, a real hussy.

Although Arend and Geertje had known each other from school, they had officially met for the first time in church. Their lasting encounter had begun with an initial shy glancing at each other, a glancing that had developed into an actual "Hi, how are you?" which in short order was followed by further chats, and a first date.

At that time already, though, she had become aware how other girls, including those in their congregation, were attracted to Arend. On church outings she could not help but notice the looks on their faces as they turned their eyes, often furtively, to her handsome boyfriend. She had become even more aware of his attraction to them during church picnics, as a number of the girls seized every opportune moment to partner with him in games, ball play, and just plain cavorting, frolicking, and sporting around with him.

In a way she could not blame them, for handsome he was what with his 1.9 meter stature, blond curly hair, innocent-looking blue eyes and, perhaps more than anything, the way he carried himself. Yet she knew that although Arend *looked* innocent, he was not unaware of his drawing power. The obvious attention they gave him stroked his ego, and had given him a sense of confidence, even of power.

Occasionally Geertje discussed this with him, but he always laughed her worries away, accusing her of being jealous. She would reluctantly admit to that, but yet there was more to her feelings than just jealousy. This was the man to whom she had emotionally committed herself, the man with whom she was planning to spend the rest of her life, the man with whom she planned to raise a family. She knew her love for him was deep and total, but was his love for her of the same strength and conviction? How would one really know? A marriage was too important to let lie lingering any doubt about the love each would have for the other, and at times she still would discuss this with him. However, any slight feeling of doubt or unease was usually laughed away, and so regardless of these slight misgivings on her part, they had married.

By and large it had been a reasonably good marriage. Therefore, when seven years ago Arend had left her, it had been extremely difficult for her to cope, and over time had put her into a deep depression from which she only now was slowly beginning to emerge. To make matters worse, two years ago, in a burst of anger, their eighteen-year old daughter Marijke had left home. In Alphen aan den Rijn, the largest city in the area, she now shared an apartment with another girl. Via the expressway across the Aarkanaal she could be reached by car in ten minutes, but in spite of that close proximity she might as well have been on a different planet – there had been little contact between Marijke and her Mom.

From where she sat in the café she could see across the plaza to the old Regthuys. Built well over four centuries ago the weight of time had actually bent the lower rows of bricks of the building into a crescent. Overhead to her right she heard the raucous squawk of a heron, and saw it light next to a *sloot*, the wide water-filled ditch that bordered the plaza. No doubt it was looking for a juicy breakfast of its own.

Just beyond the sloot, the fluffy, white flowers of a field of cotton grass stretched out to a curve in the *Oortjes Pad*, the dyke that separated the Noord- and Zuideinder plassen. These were the two large lakes that together made up the "Niewkoopse Plassen." Why the dyke was called "Oortjes Pad," or "Path of the Small Ears" she didn't have a clue. What she did know was that for as long as she could remember the narrow pathway, fit only for pedestrians and bicyclists, had been a lovers' lane. She, too, had on occasion made use of its unique and romantic location. But, she mused, that was a long, long time ago.

Paying for her coffee she shouldered her now heavy backpack, crossed another little bridge back to the dyke, and walked home again, once more making her way around a number of cows crowding the narrow path. When she arrived back home she made herself a light lunch, washed it down with a glass of wine, and watched the last fifteen minutes of a web movie on the built-in screen. But she still felt depressed, and her thoughts were elsewhere.

Although for the last two years she had been alone, this was not because she had needed to be. Several times in the past, eligible males, widowers and otherwise, had approached her with proposals of marriage or partnerships. Although tempted on one or two occasions, she had always refused them. She just couldn't help still being in love with the young man she had married some twenty years earlier. A second glass of chardonnay did not make her feel any better, and she closed her eyes. Small lines of fatigue and worry had etched themselves around her eyes, and had she been able to look at herself at that moment she would have been startled, for she looked worn, and much older than her years.

It was Sunday, two days later, another nice, sunny day. Again Geertje walked to Nieuwkoop, but this time not for groceries. This time she went for soul food. She was joined by a neighboring couple who also walked to church whenever possible. As they chatted amicably all three were careful to avoid the many cow pies on the dyke, and before long they arrived at what was formerly the old Nieuwkoop *Gereformeerde Kerk*, the Reformed Church. Years ago, due to a steadily decreasing number of church members, the congregation had merged with two other groups of worshipers, and the building currently housed one of the many eclectic *Protestante* or Protestant congregations in the country.

The building itself was one of the few remaining traditional older buildings in that area of the province of *Zuid Holland*. Destroyed by fire in the early 1900s, it had been rebuilt shortly thereafter. When the church was renovated the year previous it had been discovered that under the linoleum-covered wooden floor a marvelously old tiled floor existed that no one had known about. Subsequent to that discovery the wooden floor had been removed, and the tiled floor repaired where necessary. Also the old beautifully carved wooden pulpit was moved from the narrow end of the rectangular building to one of the long sides of it. The result of the changed interior was extraordinarily appealing, and the renovation had been photographed and written up in several magazines. Indeed, the church had become a beautiful building, a valuable tourist attraction. But at this time in her life, to Geertje it meant little.

She and her friends were greeted at the door by two of the older church members, and were handed the week's church bulletin. As usual it contained the order of the worship service together with pertinent congregational and denominational news. She sat down, and presently the band musicians marched up to the front and got ready to play. Songs lit up on the large video screen in front of the pulpit, and the small congregation began to sing. The music was loud, and a number of the praise songs she thought insipid and repetitive. She was getting a headache, and soon tired of the singing. As the band played on, and the people sang on, Geertje couldn't help but wonder if the Lord actually liked to listen to this joyful noise. In fact she wondered if the Lord was really interested in, let alone cared about, any of the goings-on in this church.

Did the Lord really care that her husband had run away from her? That her daughter had left home? For months she had been struggling with those questions, had discussed them with the Rev. Paul de Groot, the minister. But that had not helped, either. His advice had always revolved around "Just keep praying" and, "You must have faith." He didn't really seem to understand her, and comfort was just not to be gotten from him. Paul was a nice man who told nice stories in a nice church. But that's what she mostly had heard from him: nice stories; he certainly had not offered her any real, lasting comfort.

Because up till now she had not received the food for the soul she had been seeking, for a while she had been "church shopping." It had not helped. Mostly this was because in other churches she did not know anyone, and especially with the paucity of people who went to church these days any newcomer would be clamped on like a leech by elderly ladies waiting for guests to arrive, requesting a name, address and phone number where s/he could be reached for further proselytizing purposes. Together with an acquaintance she had even attended a virtual reality church in nearby Amsterdam, but this had proved to be even less helpful.

That church was one of the dozen or so in Holland run under the auspices of the virtual reality laboratory of the Swiss Federal Institute of Technology, the E.P.F.L., in Lausanne, Switzerland. After entering the building she had been guided to a seat where she was fitted with a headgear the usher proudly referred to as a new Kaiser XL50. It was a head-mounted display unit which, she was told, had a "wireless Ascension tracker with twenty-two sensors," part and parcel of something called HUMAINE, the HUman MAchine Interaction Network on Emotion.

It all had made little sense to her, and because everything she viewed in the head-display unit ultimately had been only that which existed in her own mind, the entire experience caught her up in a loop of her own despondency and gloom, and she had left with a headache, confused, and unfulfilled. And so for the last little while she had gone back to the old, familiar church environs in her own little town.

After today's service she walked home again, this time by herself. Back in the house she poured herself a glass of wine, sat down in her recliner, and began to read the bulletin. In it she also read the W.C.C. announcement with the accompanying large brown envelope. When done she put the bulletin aside, and for the so-maniest time reflected: why had her marriage failed?

Before the wedding her relationship with Arend had been great, she thought, and during the many years after the tying of the knot they had had a good time together. They liked each other's personalities, and shared many of the same interests. They could have fun together, laugh together, and play together, so what had gone wrong?

The "hussy" had been a waitress at a nearby café, where coffee as well as beer and sandwiches were served and boats could be rented. It was also a place where in the back of the establishment was a pool table were every Friday evening locals gathered to hold competitions, and Jan Renzebrink would play his old yellow-keyed, leaky Titano accordion to liven up the game and the conversation. She didn't care for the place, but Arend liked his beer and his game of pool.

At first Geertje had nothing against Arend going there, but then she could not help but notice that he began to spend more and more time at the café, sometimes not coming home till after the café had closed. Whenever she questioned him about that she always met up with sullen responses, responses that over time had begun to grow into mutual confrontations and accusations. And then, one time, he hadn't come home. It was through an acquaintance, a friend of a friend, she learned Arend had spent the night with the girl of the café.

She leaned back, took another sip of her wine, and closed her eyes. As on other occasions she asked the Lord for enlightenment, and guidance, but she did not get an answer. Where was this God who supposedly loved her? Why had both the music in church and the pastor's message left her untouched, even irritated? If God was so faithful, where was he? Why had he allowed for her marriage to go on the rocks?

After a while she got up and pensively walked around for a bit. Later she took a pen out of the small jar on the side table. Filling in the W.C.C. questionnaire she slid it into the large envelope. Still before lunch she walked over to the mailbox across the road and mailed the letter. But it did not make her feel better. As she walked back to her house a swallow deep-dived in front of her, a small tuft of straw in its bill. Spring was in the air.

CHAPTER 7

Sadiq

Sadiq's parents were black Nilotic Sudanese. Years ago, under the influence of Baptist missionaries, they had converted from Islam to Christianity, and had been baptized. For a little over a year they both had taken education courses in Juba and had become teachers at the Anglican mission school at Yei. With the birth of their only child, Sadiq, their hearts had overflowed with thanks to the God who had so blessed them. But early on there had been trouble with the new baby. Sadiq had been list-less, colicky, and had not taken well to breastfeeding. His first few years of life had been characterized by crying and frequent trips to the doctor in Juba. And then there had been a terrible natural disaster.

During an unusually wet rainy season, combined with the effects of unrestrained clear-cutting, a sudden torrent from the mountains caused a flash flood. The Bahr-el-Jebel, the 1000 km long section of the White Nile, had overflowed its banks, and together with many others both Sadiq's parents had drowned in the raging waters of the flood. Seven-year old Sadiq had been spared only because at the time of the flood he was visiting with his auntie and uncle in Juba.

Overcome with pity the latter took Sadiq into their home and hearts and raised him as their own. But then another calamity happened, as in his early twenties Sadiq was diagnosed with os-teomyelitis, an infectious bone disease that first showed up in his left leg. Sadly, and although quite uncommon, within months it had spread to his right one. The infection could not be contained, and Sadiq had to be hospitalized. He was in hospital for many months, but despite continued use of the latest infection-fighting drugs and antibiotics, ultimately, and to save his life, Sadiq had to have both legs amputated just above the knee. He was twenty-two.

It had taken the better part of a year for his wounds to heal and the stumps to harden, and then it had taken a good while longer to learn to maneuver the cart his uncle had made for him. But although the musculature in his arms had developed in tandem with the efforts he had put forth, riding the wheeled plank remained a slow and cumbersome way of locomotion. Still, the many years of practice made him move in a regular rhythm. He well recalled how it had been far slower and much more difficult to move ahead by swinging his body backwards and forwards between his arms, and therefore Sadiq did not complain.

The left front wheel had developed an awful tendency to go sideways, and every so often he had to stop and re-align it. Confined to the small contraption on wheels he had difficulty negotiating the brown dusty earth strewn with small rocks and pebbles, and the recalcitrant wheel did not help. He was glad his uncle had used castor wheels, for they worked better than the straight wheels used on the plank of one of his friends. The wheels of Sadiq's cart usually swiveled nicely, and it had only been in the last few days that the left front wheel had been acting up.

He was employed part-time by the large grocery store down the road. For them he did most of the pricing and labeling, and occasionally delivered small items to some of the elderly or infirm customers who found it difficult to negotiate the dust, pebble-strewn road that served as the main street of the village. And slowly, but steadily, he was saving up money. In another year or so, he figured, he would have enough to purchase an electric, battery-run wheelchair, and that would certainly open a new and different world for him!

From somewhere the sound of an old CD wafted into the ether. Sadiq recognized the voice of Al zol al Sameh. Even thought the lyrics were in his native Arabic, with all the modern stuff that was happening in music these days it sounded strangely foreign to Sadiq Ahmed's ears. He sat on his little cart, the large brown envelope he had picked up in church this past Sunday balanced in his lap. With heavily calloused hands he pushed himself forward towards a mailbox.

His stay with uncle and aunty in many respects had been similar to the time he had lived with his own parents. They, like them, were Christians. Moreover, uncle and aunty were staunch, active members of the S.S.F.I., the South Sudanese Friends International, a Christian organization that sought to bring the love of Jesus to the peoples of the Southern Sudan.

But now, at age twenty-seven, Sadiq had little sense left of this "love of Jesus," and rather experienced a sense of alienation from a God he really had never personally met. This was a God who not only had taken his parents, but who also had been responsible for the sickness in his legs. If God was "love," why had all this happened to him? Does "love" drown people in floods? Does "love" cause people to lose the use of their legs?

Tears pressed against his eyes, but when he stopped his cart to brush them away with the back of his hands some dirt from the road was rubbed into them, making the stinging worse. He looked around to see if anyone had seen him, but no one was near.

Here he sat, on the side of a dusty road, hot, alone, and his eyes hurt. What was he going to do with his life? In the distance a baby cried, reflecting his own inner self. A car passed by throwing up a cloud of dust, and high up in the trees and telephone wires cicadas sang their high-pitched, piercing song.

Slowly he pushed himself towards the mailbox. The sun was warm on his bare back, and except for the tumult and turmoil in his heart the entire scene was harmonious and peaceful. He stopped in front of the mailbox, reached up, and placed the envelope in the slot but, pinching it tight, did not quite let it go.

Sadiq sat like that for some time, and then pulled the envelope back. He looked around him. But for the cicadas all was quiet. Then, as if pushed by some force, he closed his eyes, and prayed. He did not really know to whom he was praying, or even that he *was* praying. But it seemed not to matter. In a stream of anguish the words, the complaints, and the hurt just flowed forth from his heart, tumbling out and, not addressed to anyone in particular, swirled around in the ether. Who would hear his cry for help?

After a while he opened his eyes, and for a moment had to think where he was. The scenery around him looked extraordinarily bright, and he had to squint to see properly. Sadiq looked at the envelope and then thought to himself, "Well, perhaps I'll just mail the letter. Who knows, perhaps it will be one of those chosen to be answered by God, and he will answer my questions, and all that has happened to me will be explained to me. If there is a God!"

Sadiq was startled by his own question, a question he had never actually asked himself before. He looked around him. Had anyone heard him? He rolled his cart back a little, away from the mailbox, and thought over what he had just asked. Was there actually a God? Did he have proof of that? He had never seen God, but all his life had prayed to him, had gone to church, and church meetings, and on many occasions had talked with his uncle and auntie about God. Until now he had never questioned the existence of God, but then again, who really knew? If he would mail the letter, would a "God" actually read it?

Still, he thought, if there were no God, how was it possible that as he sat on his cart yesterday, right by his auntie's home, he for a long time he could watch a beautifully colored butterfly emerge out of a gold-colored chrysalis, slowly pump fluid in his wings, and suddenly flutter away? And why was it that last rainy season pretty white and not red or blue flowers sprouted out of the Acacia tree in their backyard?

He next thought back on last Sunday when he sat on his cart in the aisle, at the back of the church. The minister had reminded the small congregation of the questionnaires lying on a table by the entrance, and urged anyone who felt in any way slighted by God to pick one up and mail it in. It seemed to Sadiq that when he said this he had looked right at him, and when he left after the service, making sure auntie and uncle did not see him, he picked up one of the questionnaires, and together with a large brown envelope tucked it under his shirt.

Suddenly resolute he moved his cart towards the mailbox, placed the envelope in the slot, and let go of it. The deed was done. Behind him he heard the sound of the approaching trolley that once a day picked up the mail. The cicadas continued their shrill concert as if nothing had happened.

CHAPTER 8

Sook

MV Hankyoreh, the Philippine-built Tricat, lay along the wharf of Ulleung-do harbor. The ferry lay ready to leave on its daily 100-mile trip from the island to the mainland. Its four-diesel propulsion system would make short shrift of the voyage: the ship was scheduled to moor at the wharf in the breakwater-enclosed Mukho's harbor in less than three hours. All that was needed for actual departure was the fiat of the Captain.

Ever since the opening of the port in Donghae, a little distance up the coast, Mukho's port increasingly had become fishing harbor. Built along the mountainside, Mukho's harbor side area consisted mostly of sushi- and other restaurants and stores. Together with their colorful displays and advertisements the small commercial district contrasted sharply with the somber, black rock formations behind it.

Today, over the harbor and out over the ocean, the sky looked dark and ominous, and instead of the familiar morning hustle and bustle most boats of the local fishing fleet lay still in the harbor waiting for the harbor master to give a weather update. Everyone was anxious to leave, desirous of netting a good catch of fish to be sold on the quay. However, they had been informed that a storm loomed just over the horizon, and already at the shoreline one could see waves becoming stronger and whitecaps beginning to form. Also the heat was becoming more oppressive by the hour, and the fishermen became increasingly pessimistic about the possibility of leaving.

Born in the Sea of Japan, the storm had been gathering strength for days. Named *Etau*, it had been classified as a tropical storm with potential typhoon force. Slowly but steadily it had been curving towards the Coast of the Korean peninsula, and was forecast to make landfall on the Eastern seaboard by the middle of the afternoon of the twelfth. It was 10 October, 2059.

Through special Sunday news bulletins on the Weather Network Sook had been made aware of the impending storm. Her husband was out on the island and, with her in-laws gone for two days, she was alone. Right after church today, together with some of the neighboring families, she had brought in some of the netting that lay along the small quay. Sook had not been able to do much of the heavy work. Her time was very near. But she wasn't worried so much about the netting as she was about Hyun-Ki, her husband, a supplier of specialty restaurant food. Yesterday he had left on the 10 A.M. sailing, and was scheduled to return today. But the ferry had still not arrived, and was already thirty minutes late. Nothing could have happened to it, could it?

Apprehensive, she called the harbormaster for information. He calmed her troubled spirit with the news that the ferry was going to stay over at the Ulleung--do port until the storm had blown over. With several hundreds of passengers aboard, not wanting to take a chance, the captain had decided to sit out the storm in port rather than having to battle it. Sook felt disappointed but still relieved and, as was her wont, fell into singing softly one of the many folksongs she knew. Suddenly she was overcome by a wave of unfamiliar pain in her lower back; it nearly doubled her over.

Hyun-Ki sat in the hotel restaurant on Ulleung-do. The Gwangwang was one of the better hotels on the island, certainly the largest. He had made some good sales today, and was hungry. With considerable relish he tucked into his plate of Honghap-bap, the hard--shelled mussels with rice. A waiter walked over with a portable videophone. "Mr. Hyun-Ki? Phone for you." On the small screen he saw his wife's pretty, porcelain-like face. She smiled shyly, and for the umpteenth time he was overcome with his love for her. They had been married for a little over a year, and especially with their first baby on the way their relationship had much intensified. "Hi, darling," he said, "How's things? How's the baby?" Sook then told him of her concerns about his being there when her time would come. He told her not to worry about it: he would be there.

They chatted for a few minutes. Suddenly her eyes grew big with consternation. They looked down at the same time, and both saw the widening stain. "Ooooh," exclaimed Sook, "My water just broke! What am I going to do?" Hyun-Ki's eyes, too, registered shock, but "Don't worry," he said, "I'll be there in an hour!" "But honey," Sook said, "The ferry won't be going until tomorrow, after the storm!" Hyun-Ki, suddenly in control again, said in a calm voice, "Sweetheart, don't worry. Everything will be okay. I have a way to get home." He added, "Go to one of the neighbors and ask someone to drive you to the hospital. I'll be there shortly, I promise." With that he blew her a kiss, placed the phone beside his half-eaten plate, and took the lift up to his room. In a jiffy he gathered his belongings, paid his bill, and ran out to take a cab to the harbor.

There, he looked for a familiar face, that of Cousin Henry. Spotting him in a sushi shop he told him of his urgent need. Without delay they both ran to the wharf and loosened the rope that held Henry's moored Zodiac. Although an older model, driven by a 40 horse Yanmar-powered engine, the Futura 2058 model Zodiac was one of the better known inflatables in the Virage series, and popular around the island. Checking the gasoline level and finding the tank completely filled, he donned a PFD, took the tiller, waved a quick good-bye to Henry, and veered off towards the mainland leaving a high rooster tail of spume in his wake.

A large tree, snapped off at the base by a lightning strike, had floated down some river, somewhere, many years ago. All this time the snag had bobbed in the tropical waters of the Sea of Japan, and had become almost fully waterlogged. Because of this it had begun to float vertically, the jagged end of the large log a few centimeters below the surface. Within months it would slowly, harmlessly float down to the dark depths of the ocean to stay there, preserved for centuries. Right now, however, it was one of the most feared obstacles for small boat mariners across the globe: a deadhead.

When Hyun-Ki with great speed ran into the tree it ripped open the hull of the Zodiac like a can of sardines. He was thrown down and forward, hitting the right side of his head hard on the anchor lying in the prow. Immediately water began to rush in through the long, wide gash, and quickly the boat was swamped. Hyun-Ki, unconscious, was lying face-down in the water. Within minutes he drowned.

After the storm had passed, many hours later, his body was found. It still lay confined within the floating wreckage of the Zodiac, gently rocked and caressed by the rhythmic swells of the unceasing waves.

Upon her asking for help a neighbor had indeed rushed Sook to the hospital, where in about three hours a baby-boy was born. It was pronounced to be a wonderfully healthy child, but unbeknownst to both it and its mother would have no living father. It was only two days later, after an increasingly anxious Sook asked if her husband had arrived yet, that the doctor told her the sad news.

It took many weeks for the truth to sink in, many more months for healing to begin. Instead of her husband, the baby had now become Sook's single focus in life. But something had broken inside her. The sun did not shine as brightly as before, birdsong sounded harsher, and her joy was muted. The only kind of song now passing her lips was that of a softly-sung lullaby to her child.

More and more Sook began to isolate herself. As she had stopped going to church, the only time she spoke with others was when she and her baby went for walks and met someone she knew, or when she went to the store for groceries. Her life had become a lonely one, and although almost in seclusion, she did not seem to mind. Books she had plenty, and as she loved reading she read much, re-read the books she particularly liked. But the Bible was one book she no longer read.

Lee Seung Jun was the new pastor at the small Mukho Baptist congregation. Fresh from seminary, single, and very enthusiastic about his first charge, he worked hard especially with the young folks in the church. Not even thirty years old, this wasn't too difficult for him – being close to the age of most of the young people in the church their questions were similar to the ones he not so long ago had faced himself.

Besides his involvement with the ministry the young preacher had one more abiding passion: astronomy. Already when a child, lying on his back in the grass and armed with a set of binoculars, he had patiently explored the constellations and planets. Over time he graduated from his binoculars, first to a three-inch telescope, later to a four-inch equatorially mounted refractor, and had acquired an impressive overall knowledge of the night sky.

Pastor Lee Seung Jun had become the new pastor of the church about three months after Sook had lost her husband, and therefore had not known Hyun-Ki personally. But although Sook did not come to his church, through talks with other members of the congregation he knew who she was. He thought her aloof in her demeanor, and a somewhat mysterious figure. But his interest in her was piqued, for he also found her attractive…

One day he was walking in the shopping district by the harbor when Sook, holding her little child by the hand, was walking along the same side of the street coming towards him. He stopped, and introduced himself. They did not have a lengthy conversation, but long enough for Lee Seung Jun to invite her to come to church this coming Sunday. Sook told him she did not have time, and he did not press the matter. But in the process of the meeting he had looked into her sad eyes. And was incurably in love.

As often before, that night sleep for Sook wouldn't come, and thoughts whirled around in her head. She got up, and had a piece of chocolate. The meeting with the Baptist pastor had confused her, and somehow left her feeling at odds with herself. She certainly had no intention of going back to that church, but had to admit the minister had been a nice person to meet and speak with.

The encounter with the pastor reminded her of the W.C.C. questionnaire she had placed into her file some time back; retrieving it she noted she had already filled it in. She placed the form in the brown envelope, laid it by her other mail to be posted, and went back to bed. In the morning all letters were mailed.

That same night Lee Seung Jun sat on his balcony and looked at the Andromeda galaxy. Located at the northeastern corner of the Great Square of Pegasus it was visible even to the naked eye. He knew that through the scope several of its beautiful double stars could be seen, stars that to a careful observer would relinquish their startling blue-green beauty.

Tonight, however, his telescope stayed inside, his thoughts wandering to the galaxy's mythological main character: Andromeda, the beautiful daughter of King Cepheus and Queen Cassiopeia. Because the Queen had boasted about her daughter's beauty, the Roman god Neptune decreed that Andromeda should be chained to a rock by the seashore so to be made prey for a terrible sea monster. It was a good thing Perseus had turned the monster into stone, and the story had a happy ending.

Lee Seung Jun, too, was desirous of rescuing a beautiful Andromeda from a sad fate. He, too, wished for a happy ending, and looking beyond the stars, he sighed.

Far above him Capella, the "Goat star," absolutely winked at him…

CHAPTER 9

Derek

It was late morning, and Derek O'Connor slowly walked along the narrow lane. It was a typical mist-shrouded day. Low-hanging clouds lay over his fields, making for a landscape of vague shapes and secret hollows. The giant Guango tree he knew to be at the edge of his field was obscured from view, and with the gloom the weather had cast over this part of the Dry Harbour Mountains even the birds in the hedgerows along the lane were quieter than normal. A Streamer-tailed hummingbird, flashing its iridescent green plumage right in front of Derek, skimmed passed him over the drystone walls alongside the lane, startling him out of his mournful mood.

For Derek's mood was dark: already a widower for many years, four weeks earlier Teddy and James, his twin boys, had been killed. Some years back David, the oldest son of the owner of the Kirkvine Bauxite refinery in Nain, had befriended the two boys. He had been taking flying lessons for several years, and had obtained a bona fide pilot's license. On his birthday before last his dad had bought him a small plane, an old but revamped four-seat Piper Cherokee. On this occasion David had to go on business for his Dad in Port-Au-Prince, and had asked his twin friends to keep him company on the trip. They were delighted at the prospect, and taking off work from the mine for a few days they happily agreed to come along.

The plane never arrived in Haiti. After more than a week of

searching by Coast Guard and Jamaican police helicopters no wreckage had been spotted, the search was called off, and all three boys were assumed drowned.

The low overhanging clouds together with the fog well reflected Derek's gloomy mood. He turned and went back to the farmhouse. The building looked bright and clean: just six weeks ago his boys had newly white-washed the entire house and several of the outbuildings. His boys had been so young, so promising. Why had life been so terribly unfair?

Just fifty-eight years old, why would he now have to face it alone? Not that the people of his church hadn't been good to him. Parcels had arrived via courier as well as regular mail service, and he had been supplied with food to last him for well over a month. But what good was that to him having to eat it all by himself?

In an attempt to bring comfort, he had received much regular as well as electronic mail from his church brothers and sisters. Occasionally two or three had even come down in the flesh to pray with him. But to Derek their words had been just words, words that washed over him and left him as empty as before. How could anyone possibly know how it felt to lose two children at once?

Derek belonged to the "Disciples of Christ" electronic church based in Kingston. Their services under senior pastor/televangelist Jack Weinberg (Jaacov Weinberg was a Christianized Jew) were broadcast three times weekly over the C.V.M. television station in Kingston. For years Derek and his family had faithfully sat down in front of the large screen each time there was a service. It had been good. But now things were different.

After the loss of his boys he had continued watching the services for a while, looking for comfort, but had found none. Instead it had been for him a lonely and largely useless experience, one that only seemed to make him feel worse. And sing along with the choral group he could not either, for whenever he tried tears would well up in his eyes, and he would choke up; he knew that he would never be able to sing or laugh again.

These days he walked a lot, walk, and ask "Why? What had he done? What had he done to deserve this? Why had God been so cruel to him?" Some weeks back he simply decided to stop watching the church services. By no stretch of the imagination could he any longer see himself as a "Disciple of Christ." His family was gone, that was all that mattered. The church chapter in his life was closed. For good.

When he arrived at his farmhouse he walked around the large egg-shaped Poui tree, now in full flower, and went inside. From a side-table he retrieved an old church bulletin, and took from it the envelope and form he knew to be inside. As he sat down by his ancient roll-top desk he filled in the questionnaire and enclosed it in the self-addressed stamped brown envelope.

He walked the short distance to the mailbox, mailed the letter, and went back home. Once there, he sat by the kitchen table, lay his head on his folded arms, and wept. The cuckoo clock in the kitchen cuckooed the noon hour.

Far away in Kingston the Rev. Weinberg, somewhat belatedly, had read about the accident in the Jamaica Gleaner, the daily paper. He had not at first known the boys involved were members of his television congregation. After having been made aware of the facts of the case, however, he determined to discuss the matter at next month's plenary session of overseers so that from now on matters like these would be brought to his attention immediately for him to act upon.

The Reverend, a compassionate man, decided to visit Derek, to have a chat with him and, if given the opportunity, to pray with him and attempt to bring comfort. His television congregation was a large one, and most individual needs were met through the appointed overseers in charge of the various sections in the country. But this case, Pastor Weinberg thought, needed special attention. A father's loss of two children at the same time was a devastating thing, and the accident saddened him deeply.

Carefully he drove his old station wagon along the winding road through Spanish Town and May Pen, and when close to

Mandeville turned north towards Villa Bella and Christina near where Derek lived.

The latter was at work in his garden, was surprised at the visit, but welcomed Pastor Jack warmly. He offered the travel-weary pastor a cold drink, which was gratefully accepted. And then they talked. And talked some more. And then they went for a walk along the narrow lane, past the drystone walls, and turned off into the field. As they walked to the end of the fairly extensive property, all the way to the Guango, Derek spoke of his feelings, his anger towards God, and he broke down crying. Pastor Jack was very much touched by the man's sorrow. He, too, cried, and at some point both men together hugged, and wept. After that they slowly walked back to the farmhouse.

Back there they had tea and talked some more, this time about the weather and the price of vegetables. Some time later, when saying their goodbyes, Derek stopped the preacher and from his pantry carried to the station wagon a large box with canned and dried foods. "For the Mustard Seed," he said, and Pastor Jack gladly accepted the gift; the Mustard Seed was one of the more important services for the poor and destitute with which the church was regularly involved.

As the car drove away Derek went back into the house. Somehow he seemed to walk ever so slightly straighter than he had done in some time, and there definitely was a hint of a spring in his step.

CHAPTER 10

Pedro

Not paying any attention to the speed limit, Padre Vargas drove his '48 Braga along the R. Maria Paula. With tires squealing the older but still funky carbon fiber Portuguese import exited from the expressway, turned right at R. Santo Amara, and laid a strip of rubber as it screeched to a stop in the designated parking area of the Igreja de São Francisco de Assis, his home church. Padre Pedro Vargas had driven his hydrogen-fuelled car uncharacteristically hard, even somewhat recklessly, along the underground twelve-lane expressway. Because Padre Pedro was deeply troubled.

Two months earlier he had been transferred from a cute, comfortable small town church in the Guarapuava diocese to the large one here in São Paulo. Not that he missed small town politics or the hot interior climate. He took pleasure in the esthetically pleasing well-preserved baroque architecture of his new ecclesiastical home, and got along well with the other priests. He liked the way masses and services were conducted, and even had several good friends amongst the lay-brothers who for many years already had run the other half of the catholic services. No, Padre Pedro was happy and fulfilled in his calling, except for one thing. But that one thing posed an almost insurmountable problem for a priest in the current Roman Catholic Church: Padre Pedro was in love – with a girl.

Althea sat on a straight chair before the children in her

classroom. Crouched at her feet some two dozen twelve- to thirteen- year olds waited expectantly as she began, "You know, in the Atlantic, beyond the beach by Santos, live small whales called dolphins. They mostly have a longer snout than the large whales that we studied last month, and there are many interesting stories about these dolphins. Some say they help people who have fallen overboard a ship to get back to land again; others believe they have special gifts making both mentally and physically challenged children feel happy. Still others say they are as smart as people. I don't know if any of that is true, but what I do know is they are unusually bright and playful mammals that have a great way of communicating with each other."

"Now there is one special kind of dolphin that lives in the Amazon, far north from here, and the people there tell interesting stories about them. They say that these dolphins, the *botos*, can take on human form. And whenever they do they always dress themselves immaculately in white clothing and go to parties to dance with the youngest and most beautiful girls there. They lure them outside where they hug and kiss them, but always make sure to return to the river just before dawn. Why that is, nobody knows. It is not that girls should ever be fooled by a boto, because one can always recognize a boto by its slightly fishy smell and the hole in the top of its head. You can understand, therefore, why a boto often uses a very strong deodorant, and wears a hat!"

Just before questions would come about the strange tale with the quirky ending the school buzzer buzzed, and the class emptied. Althea sat alone, and smiled about the legend. It was a tale she herself had often heard when she was a child – it was a story still popular today. But then her thoughts went to her own sweet dolphin, the forbidden love of her life. And he for sure wasn't a boto. He was a priest called Pedro. I all had happened so suddenly.

She had been to confession, and had been forcefully struck by the resonant, warm baritone voice of the priest on the other side of the screen. Who was he? He had never been her confessor before. Then, after one early mass, she had watched this handsome, tall priest go into the confessional accompanied by an older woman who was doing the confessing. Somehow she suspected it just might be him, and when the woman left she decided to go in, too. She thought of something to confess, and quickly came up with the notion she had not been praying enough. After all, one could always confess to something like that!

Once inside the confessional she definitely recognized the voice: it was him. After the assigned penance she left quickly, flushed, and a bit embarrassed. Upon inquiry from a friend she later learned the new priest's name was Father Pedro Vargas. And Althea was totally and desperately in love with him.

On leaving the confessional Padre Vargas had seen the lissome girl walk away, and his eyes had strayed to the graceful and alluring swinging of her hips. Throughout the rest of the day the scene had kept him from concentrating on the things on which he really should have been concentrating. Today, stronger than ever before, he felt in him again the struggle, the conflict between his maleness and his professed commitment to celibacy.

Weeks went by, and on several occasions he noticed the girl's presence in the sanctuary. They glanced at each other, but that was all. And then the unthinkable happened. One weekday afternoon he was reading his breviary on a park bench in the Parque Anhagabaú, a few blocks away from church, when he saw her. He raised his hand and waved at her, and she walked over and sat beside him. He placed his breviary on the bench and covered it with his hand. As he did, he lightly touched the girl's hand which rested beside her on the seat. Neither of them moved their hand away.

Padre Pedro made some innocuous comments about the park and the flowers, to which she responded with similar small talk about the weather. Then they both fell silent. But their hands were still touching, and through them now coursed a current so strong that nothing needed be said. Awed by the force of the flow they silently communicated a love, a meeting of souls so powerful, that small shivers ran across the backs of both of them. And then Padre Pedro's hand left the breviary, and placed it over hers. Althea didn't draw away, and they both knew that something had happened that would have a tremendous impact on both their lives, something that would forever change them.

But Padre Pedro was not just anybody. His original commitment to the priesthood had been the result of years of deep thought, meditation and prayer. It had not been a lightly made decision, but one that had flowed from a heart deeply devoted to the Lord and the church, done voluntarily, and never under any kind of duress. But now, unexpectedly, Althea had come into his life in a manner he never before would have thought possible. What should he do?

In many of the nights that followed he wrestled with his conscience, a conscience that had to deal with a terrible dilemma as the vow to live the celibate life of the priest was suddenly counterbalanced by his need for a different vow, a vow to forever be true to the other love of his life, his Althea. Because of the turmoil in his heart, sleep at night began to evade him more and more. But he was not only losing his sleep but also his appetite, and some of his fellow priests began to notice there was something definitely wrong with Brother Pedro. Of course when they questioned him about his health there was no way he could possibly tell them what the problem was. However, because of their expressed concerns, he began to realize he needed help.

After much contemplation and discussing of the situation with an equally concerned Althea he decided to seek audience with his Bishop, Bishop Antônio Zerbini. Within the week the request was granted.

It was with leaden steps Padre Pedro drove up to the Bishop's residence, and rang the bell. The kindly bishop himself opened the door. Soon they were seated in some comfortable chairs, and Padre Pedro laid his problem before the Bishop.

Needless to say the discussion lasted for a long time. Initially the Bishop reminded him of the serious consequences he would

have to face should he break his priestly vow, but then the talks
went into the more reasoned details of the matter. He quoted a
number of passages from Scripture supporting celibacy for the
priesthood, and mentioned that these texts were further shored
up by past Papal pronouncements. But the young priest had also
been studying the matter, and reminded him that Peter, the first
Pope, had also been married and that until the twelfth century
marriages for priests in the church were normal, and allowed.
Why, he asked the bishop, had that changed?

The Bishop responded by reminding Pedro about the commitment of his vow, and asked why *that* had changed. He continued
his response by pulling from a drawer in his desk a copy of the
1965 Vatican II encyclical, the *Optatium Totius* which, in part,
stated that "Virginal consecration to Christ is of greater excel-
lence than Christian marriage." Padre Pedro, in turn, responded
by reacted to this by referring to a passage in I Timothy 4, which
states in strong language that any such teachings are human
teachings, and are not of the Lord.

The discussion simply ended in an impasse: the Bishop was
not able to have Pedro change his thinking on the matter, and
the talk was ended. The Bishop asked Pedro to stay a little longer
and have a glass of wine with him. They spoke some more, and
the Bishop even discussed some aspects of his own struggles with
celibacy. But, he said, he had made the vow, and had never been
able to find it in him to break it. After all, he said gently, a vow is
a vow. This, of course, was precisely Padre Pedro's problem, but
one that simply was overshadowed by the love he felt the Lord
had put in his heart for the pretty schoolteacher.

The Bishop and the young priest then prayed, asking for the
Lord's guidance in both their lives, after which they shook hands,
and parted amicably; there was no residue of anger on either side.
On the way home Pedro thought back on the discussion. He
knew that partially because of the celibacy policy of the church
there had been a steady decline in seminary enrollment for the
priesthood, something that had already begun in the early 1900s.

To be sure, thought Padre Pedro, celibacy might well be right for some, like Bishop Zerbini. However, it had become clear that this was not what the Lord wanted for *him*. The strong, prayerfully considered conviction helped him keep at bay any guilt he might have otherwise harbored.

Once home he sat down in his favorite chair. He was exhausted, mentally, and physically. He leaned his head back against the headrest, closed his eyes, and momentarily fell asleep.

After a good hour he awoke, and planning to do some reading he picked up one of the two Bibles that lay on the floor beside him. He absentmindedly opened the book, found himself looking at the thirtieth chapter of Numbers, and noticed that many years earlier, when still in seminary, he had underlined the first two verses. They read,

"This is what the Lord commands:
When a man makes a vow to the Lord
or takes an oath to obligate himself by a pledge,
he must not break his word but must do everything he said."

Padre Pedro sat up straight, and the blood drained from his face. He stood up, and looked around him. This was almost as if God himself was directly speaking at him! He got up, walked around, and looked out the window. Then he walked around some more, and looked out the other window. He sat down, and looked at the passage again. Suddenly he reasoned: the book of Numbers is in the Old Testament, so that text does not count anymore, right? That just was an old law, and Jesus had come and had fulfilled the law! He, Padre Pedro, did not have to abide by that text, did he?

But his rationalizing did not help, and still suddenly he knew what he had to do. He walked up to the videophone, called Althea in her classroom, and asked her to drop by after school. On the screen she noticed the lines of fatigue on his face, and immediately wondered if something was wrong. Knowing he had been at the Bishop's she asked the question, but he did not elaborate, and Althea, worried now, agreed to drop by after school.

She let herself in with the key he had given her. Pedro was seated on the antique jacaranda *conversadeira*, the double backed armchair he had taken along from Guarapuave. She sat down beside him, looked at him with a worried frown on her face, saying nothing, waiting for Pedro to begin talking. Pedro did. He told her he had to break off their relationship, gave her the reason, and subsequently begged her forgiveness for having started it.

Althea said nothing. In some strange way she had expected it, had been worried about their relationship from the moment he had told her he was going to see Bishop Zerbini. She did not even argue, or break down into tears. She looked at him with the saddest eyes he had ever seen or would ever see again, and left. There was a strange, terrible ache in his chest.

Later that week Padre Pedro took one of the large left-over W.C.C. envelopes from a stack lying in the sacristy. A short while later he filled in the form contained in it, went out, and mailed it. Hopefully his letter would be chosen by the selection committee for God to explain why his faithful servant Pedro had been so abandoned by reason, and had been pitched on the horns of such a brutal dilemma.

CHAPTER 11

Tala

Just past St. Stephen's gate the Bab Sitt Maryam ended and the Jalla Beena began. The corridor, fenced on both sides, consisted of a newly constructed eight-lane expressway that joined the old Derekh Ha-ofel and Ma'aleh Shalom roads. Its terminus was almost immediately after what had been the old "Green Line" east of Gaza city. The idea of a corridor connecting the two sections of Palestine through Israel had come from another corridor used after World War II, when right through East German proper it had connected the city of West Berlin to the remainder of West Germany. From the West it had served as that city's only access by land.

Its naming had been a bone of contention for some time, but in the end the inoffensive name "Jalla Beena," meaning "Let's Go" in Arabic, had been decided upon as a non-controversial one that shouldn't, and in fact didn't, offend either Israeli or Palestinian sensitivities.

As the bus traveled east along the Jalla Beena, Tala Abu Rahma sat in the back and stared out the window, his mind momentarily on his friend Jamal al-Durrah and his wonderful new wife. Their wedding had been last week. As Jamal's best friend he had been invited but had not been able to attend, for when he drove home from work the day before the wedding he had experienced severe chest pains. Well aware of his heart condition he hadn't wanted to take any chances, and had quickly checked himself into the Ahri Arab hospital.

Upon arrival he was stabilized immediately, and all manner of tests and scans were performed. The result was something he knew already: his heart was not functioning well; this was the third time this year he had had this kind of episode. Some twelve years ago he had been the recipient of a heart transplant, and knew that to have yet another one to replace this one would be highly unlikely. Now, after a five-day stay, he was on the way back to the West Bank, back to speak with another, even older friend about the condition of his heart . . . .

After many decades of warring with Israel peace had finally arrived in the Middle East. The beginning of the peace process could be traced back to the death, fifty-six years earlier, of Palestinian president Yasser Arafat. Arafat had been much loved by the Palestinians, but regarded as controversial at best by most others, especially the Israeli. The intifada had ended, and in AD 2048 the state of Palestine had been officially declared.

By odd coincidence this had occurred exactly 100 years after the state of Israel had gained its independence; Tala had been twenty-one at the time. It was also the same year he had received his heart transplant, and had converted from Islam to Christianity.

At first both Tala's new heart and faith had given him much joy. He had been able to play soccer again without becoming exhausted in minutes, and he thrived on the freedom the Christian faith appeared to bring him. But now he wasn't so sure anymore – it seemed that both his heart and his faith in a Christian god were failing him. After all, if the Christian god was all-powerful, why hadn't he been healed permanently?

At the time of his conversion, now years ago, his old school friend Omar had been extremely upset with him. He had warned him that should he persist in rejecting Islam, especially when he had grown up in it and had consciously accepted it, he had better be prepared for a tough session dealing with accountability in the courts of Allah, in the Hereafter. The Arabic word for "unbelief" was *kufr*, and because he had rejected Islam his friend had called him a "kafir." At the time the epithet had stung him deeply, but after a while the hurt had passed, and today only a small scar remained.

He looked outside. Traffic surged by at speeds much faster than that of the bus, and through the window he saw fleeting images of others en route to Jerusalem. Tala looked forward to seeing his friend, and to talk with him. They had always had a great relationship, even during school days.

He recalled how he and Omar had played soccer for hours on end, usually in the small plaza in front if Omar's hours, often kicking the ball until dark. But both Omar and he were not just soccer friends. Even more so than he and Jamal, he and Omar had been very close, soul mates, even, who together could discuss politics, matters of love, and matters of faith. And so Tala was not just going to see a friend, but in a real sense was going to see his alter ego. And that would be good, for he knew that although they had been apart for a long time he right away would be able to connect with him about a truly pressing matter, the matter of his commitment to the Christian God.

Tala looked at his watch; in another half hour he would be in Jerusalem. He peered out the window at the roadside fence, but quickly looked away. The pattern of the screen melded into a continuous mesh that pressed on his eyes in a headachy fashion. Instead he closed his eyes and thought about his destination: the divided Jerusalem. Tortured city, he thought; what all it over the centuries had gone through. In a way, he thought, Jerusalem was a little bit like himself. He, too, had gone through a number of difficult experiences and, like Jerusalem, he felt divided, too.

On the one hand, he mused, the Christian experience had been a positive, happy one. Especially in the beginning he had felt fulfilled in his newly found faith. The friends he had at the "Loaf and Fishes" church had given him good reason to feel that way, too; they had been truly caring, and especially with his health issues and hospitalization had shown themselves to be real follow-ers of Christ. They loved him, and he loved them. But because of his ailing heart there was also this continued nagging doubt about his commitment to Christianity. For if Jesus could heal a withered hand, why could he not heal a withered heart?

It was that question that had begun to haunt him more and more, so much so that he made up his mind to press the issue. The year previous, already well before his last stay in hospital, the oft-televised Greek faith healer Alec Simitis had come to the large soccer stadium in Gaza. Tala, too, had gone, hoping for healing. It had not happened. When towards the end of the service the Rev. Simitis invited all the sick and infirm to come to the front, he had gone along with the attendants in the aisles and was guid-ed to the stage. There, in an all encompassing Apostolic Blessing, the healer had stretched out his hands of the hundreds gathered, and pronounce them healed.

But Tala had not felt anything. He had not felt even a small surge of Holy-Spirit-Heat course through his body as others re-ported happening to them. In between the sea of waving hands, closed eyes and the many "Speakings in the Spirit" he felt oddly out of place, and wanted out, and pushing his way through the crowd he left the stadium.

When close to the hotel where he was staying he tried to jog the last part. But he became scared, and had to stop quickly as the pain of his angina just became too pronounced. That night was also the first time in a long while that he had begun thinking back on his previous Muslim faith, the mosque he attended, where he often went not only on Fridays, but also mid-week. He thought about the prayer mats, and the daily prayers, and Ramadan, and the friends he had then. And especially he thought back to his bosom buddy, Omar. If only he could talk with him!

The next day he had put deed to the thought and had video-phoned him, inviting himself. Omar had been overjoyed. On the phone he had told Omar about his health problems, but did not give him any details about the doubts he had about his faith life.

Still, in the inside pocket of his jacket, he had taken along from church a large brown envelope with a form in it to be filled in and mailed to the World Council of Churches head office. Just in case...

He looked forward to talking with Omar, although he was chagrined he could not have a game of soccer with him; he'd be winded in minutes. But perhaps they could just kick the ball around a bit, and he could play goalie! Omar was waiting for him up at the bus terminus in the Palestinian section. He had only a vague idea why Tala was coming to see him, just knew about his health situation. He loved his friend, and felt deeply sorry for him.

After a long time of separation both friends were overjoyed to meet again. They kissed, and went for a long-lasting late lunch. And talked. Tala spoke of his doubts and frustrations, and Omar listened patiently. After many hours it became clear they had come to a common understanding, for the talking stopped, and they held hands. When from a nearby minaret the call was issued for prayer, they both were seen to go to an especially reserved area of the restaurant to pray. And, there, for the first time in many years, Tala, too, bowed to the ground in the familiar *salat*.

Afterwards, in a nearby bookstall, Omar bought his old friend a brand-new Qur'an. Later in the day, before his friend, Tala affirmed a renewed allegiance to Allah with a devoutly spoken *la ilaha illallah Muhammad-ur-Rasulullah*, and his spiritual transformation was complete.

Officially wanting to close off one part in his life and starting a new one, early next morning Tala left the hotel to get a cup of coffee and something to eat. He took along with him the large brown envelope to place in a mailbox along the way. It was windy, and raining. At a mailbox, as he wanted to slip the envelope into the receptacle, a small gust of wind hit it and it slipped out off his hand into a mud puddle. He picked it up, shook the water and the muddy spots off the envelope, and placed the letter in the mail slot. Pulling up the collar of his jacket he bent into the wind, and went for his coffee.

CHAPTER 12

Louisa

It was Friday afternoon. A watery late-spring sun tried to worm its way through the closed windows. Close to eighty students in the class theatre looked at Vivian Holwerda, Associate Professor of English, who stood behind her desk and reminded the awaiting students of something they already knew: the final fifteen minutes of the lecture were going to be taken up by a verb quiz, a previously announced timed ten minute affair.

The professor's severe hairdo culminating in a tight bun was quite representative of the course: a severely difficult, tightly organized course in English grammar. The monitors inside the students' desks came on, and the test was on.

The first part Louise thought relatively easy – it counted for 16% of the test. She had to give an example each of the three different kinds of compound verbs, the two different voices, plus one each of a linking, transitive and intransitive verb. That part she finished quickly. But then she looked at the second part, worth 84%, and her eyes glazed over. Having studied well over two hundred principal parts of strong and weak irregular verbs, she still was not prepared for what she saw now. The exacting, uncompromising Vivian Holwerda had simply outdone herself:

Select from the following eight words or non-words those that correctly complete the sentences below.

   1)   lie
   2)   laying

3) lieing
4) lay
5) layed
6) lain
7) lying
8) laid

The Chicken

The chicken is ___ down because she is going to___ an egg. Yesterday she ___ down, too, but no eggs were ___. Had she ___ down longer she might have ___ several eggs. Perhaps she will ___ down again tomorrow and be ___ some more eggs.

Hole in One

Yesturday the ___ of the land was favorable to the construction of a golf course. However, after the appearance of a large sink hole the drastically changed ___ of the land made a new course unlikely.

Too Tired

Because I am tired I am going to ___ down. Yesterday I ___ down, too. Had I not ___ down I wouldn't have had the strength to ___ the brick on the shelf. I ___ it there today because I ___ it there before. It is still ___ there now.

Money

"___ the money on the table," said Bill to Matthew, "Don't let it ___ around. It's been ___ on the counter too long; someone must have ___ it there by mistake. They should have known better that to ___ it on the counter."

With her laser pen Louisa placed what she thought were the correct numbers in the fill-ins. What a difficult exercise this last part had been. Out of hundreds of principal parts of verbs Holwerda had picked two of the most confusing ones and mixed

its contents. Assured that her parents would not mind for her to use it she filled it in, answered the questions that were posed, placed the form inside the brown envelope, and took it to her room. Shortly after her parents came home.

Louisa enjoyed dinner with them, but did not tell them what had happened. Of course her parents had quickly noticed that something was awry, but had the sense and sensitivity not to ask. Shortly after dinner they drove Louisa back to the college. She kissed her parents goodbye, walked to her dorm, and on the way placed the brown envelope in one of the campus mailboxes. Gwen wasn't home, and as it was already late Louisa went to bed. She had a restless night, and when she awoke next morning Gwen's bed was still empty. Again she sharply felt the pain of the hurt Gwen had put upon her.

She showered and dressed. When finished she went to her desk and from a drawer took out a large piece of pink bubble-gum. She closed the dorm door behind her and went for a long walk, chewing away as she went. Who'd need God anyway?

CHAPTER 13

Wes and Sara

With a raucous squawk the Brown Skua dived from the rock formation on the south side of the colony, sailed over the viewing platform, and landed on the rocky beach opposite the visitor centre. Wes Butler had just arrived, and leaned over the fence in time to see the bird pounce on a sickly Blue Penguin, immediately beginning to tear it apart. The poor Blue didn't even struggle.

It was early morning. For some reason the little penguin had not been able to reach its burrow last night and, helpless on the rocks, had attracted the hungry Skua. The Jaeger held the dead bird down with its talons, and with its fierce hooked bill tore at the flesh. Penguin feathers flew left and right. It kept at it for about ten minutes as three crows on nearby rocks waited impatiently for a morsel. They made their presence known by cawing loudly and hopping from one rock to another desperate to get at some of the scraps. Suddenly, with a flash of its white primaries and a disdainful squawk directed at the quarreling crows, the sated Skua flew off over the ocean, and the crows moved in.

Wes walked up to the visitor centre, unlocked the door, and went inside. The day had just begun, and already he had witnessed the death of one of the animals he loved, an unhappy start to a day just begun. And Wes was dispirited already.

It was only last week he and his wife Sara had been told by their GP some truly sad news. Sara, in her first trimester, had learned that the life that was growing within her was not the kind of wholly well child for which they had prayed and hoped. They had followed up on a friend's suggestion to have some tests done to assure a safe and happy pregnancy, and afterwards had learned there was a problem with the baby: they were informed that the baby would be born with Down's syndrome.

Wes went to his small office. It was crammed full with papers, articles, photographs and books. Most had to do with Blue Penguins and the New Zealand avifauna. Wes was an expert on this penguin, the smallest of the seventeen species that existed. He sat down on a computer chair and grabbed a magazine out of the magazine rack. It was the latest copy of the SPCA, an organization of which both he and his wife were members. Its international motto, "We Speak for Those Who Cannot Speak for Themselves," superimposed over a photograph of a beautifully photographed Tieke, one of the ubiquitous wattlebirds, was emblazoned on the cover in bright blue letters.

He had just begun to leaf through the magazine when the videophone flashed. It was Sara. He could see she was crying, and in some distress. When he asked her what the problem was she didn't want to tell him; in spite of the fact he had left only an hour earlier she insisted he come home right away. He shilly-shallied and told her he couldn't leave just like that, but in the end promised he would try to get one of the other assistants to fill in for him. So said so done, and fortunately Mark, one of his colleagues, was found willing to help out. Subsequently he called Sara back on the videophone and told her he'd be home soon.

Within about forty minutes he walked into his bungalow on Torridge Street, where Sara met him with a tear-streaked face. She began crying again, and between sobs told him she had decided, after all, to abort the baby.

Wes was dumbfounded. What was this about all of a sudden? True, earlier on they had fleetingly discussed this option, but had rejected it. Suddenly this. Sara sat down on the floor in front of the recliner, and Wes sat down in front of her, took her hands in his, and looked at her. She appeared really distraught. What had brought on this abrupt change of mind?

It turned out she had been watching a television program dealing with just such children. It had shown how nearly all of them could function really well in society. Many had meaningful positions, some were even well-paid actors, and of this latter group a film-clip was shown which had indeed been most impressive. It was also mentioned that nearly all such children were extremely thoughtful, friendly, and fun-loving, attentive to those who loved them and cared for them, in other words, they were simply nice people to be around.

However, during the course of the program it was also brought to the fore that although all these were positive characteristics, there were specific problems associated with Down syndrome children. Included in these were high incidence of mild to moderate retardation, and the significant possibility of them contracting one or more of a broad spectrum of infections. This fact Sara had not known, and it had given her pause. But in the course of the program several other concerns were brought to the fore, concerns of which some she herself had already thought about

How would a Down syndrome child be accepted in school and other social environments? Would such a child ever be able to have a meaningful relationship with a person of the opposite gender, and would it ever become fully independent? Can I totally love a child like that, be fully committed to it, and accept whatever cost, both emotional and financial, will be involved? What would such a child do to my and my husband's relationship? And so perhaps the most critical question of all: was it really fair to the *child* to bring it into the world?

All morning these and other questions had piled up in her heart. They had caused her to face her own weaknesses and multiplied the doubts the pregnancy was bringing her. Eventually, later in the morning, it all had come together with the conviction that she simply could not face the challenge of such a baby, and the deeply troubled Sara called Wes.

Wes tried to comfort his wife, and put his arms around her knees. But he, too, was deeply disturbed. Why had God allowed this to happen? They had tried for so long to have a baby, and finally Sara had become pregnant. Was this the best God could do for them?

Together they discussed the program Sara had watched, the points that were made, and the questions that were raised about Down syndrome children. Although during earlier general discussions especially Wes, but also Sara, had pronounced abortions as anathema for Christian people, today Sara's bringing it up brought the topic forcefully to the fore once again. And the longer they talked, the more Wes began to sympathize with his wife's feelings. After all, especially during the early years it was likely she would end up having to do most of the care-giving, and by the looks of it that was not going to be a sinecure. In the end, suddenly resolute, Wes stood up, took his wife by the hand, hugged her, and told her an abortion would be arranged. But in bed later that night Wes couldn't help but think back on the S.P.C.A. motto and, in connection with the planned termination of the pregnancy, the irony of it all.

An appointment with an abortion clinician next day resulted in a set time for the procedure to take place later that week. Both felt apprehensive about it, but were assured by the clinician that in case of an unwanted pregnancy this was a common course of action with little risk to the mother. Later that week the operation was performed, and everything went as planned, and hoped.

For the first time in a long while, the following Sunday Wes did not go to church. The reason for this was that in spite of their decision to have the baby aborted, two days before the date this was to happen, Wes and Sharon had visited Dr. Vermont, their minister at the Oamaru Presbyterian church. They had not felt entirely comfortable about their decision, and had looked for his affirmation, his blessing on the planned procedure. Matters had not gone as they had hoped.

Dr. Vermont had serious concern about their plans. He felt

that for a confessing child of the Lord, the Giver of life, it would seem the wrong thing to do, and would likely bring sadness, and regret. He attempted to have Wes and Sara see their baby as a gift of God, and expressed the view that for God to give them a special needs child was because they themselves were special, and had been especially chosen for the task of raising it. Towards the close of their visit Dr. Vermont had prayed with them, asking the Lord for guidance in their lives, especially in the important decision they were about to make. But Wes had become quite upset, and had left with only the curtest of a spoken goodbye.

While church was on, Sara was reading, and Wes watched an Australian football game on the television. After the game he went to the side table and picked up the previous week's church bulletin. Absentmindedly he looked through it, and noticed the W.C.C. form. He had seen it before, but at the time had found no need to bother with it. Now matters were different. Determined, he called Sara, and seated by the kitchen table together they filled in the form. Sealing it they placed it in the postage-paid envelope provided, went for a brief walk in the sunshine, and mailed the letter on the way.

CHAPTER 14

Yahaya

As the fishing boat came closer to his village Yahaya began to see the houses along the water's edge ever more clearly outlined against the darkening sky. This was the fishing village of Menkabong, a collection of homes born out of need. When poor Malaysian fishermen had simply not been able to afford housing in town, and would have had no possible way to pay property taxes, they had built a fishing village on the tidal flats. After all, nobody could tax them there!

All homes in the village were built on poles made out of iron wood, a hard wood that in the salt water of the South China Sea would last for as long as sixty years. The homes were connected by narrow planked roads. In the center and on top of these pathways ran PVC pipes that supplied everyone with potable water. Electricity had been put in years ago, and the education of children was taken care of in a school built on the nearby shore. Still, even with all this relative modernization, many homes had buffalo horns on their roofs. This was because of the Balang Balang.

The Balang Balang was thought to be a community of evil consisting of a head from which dangled long entrails. It was believed the Balang Balang went around looking for openings in village roofs through which it could enter. Once inside, it would suck the amniotic fluid from pregnant women, killing both the woman and the baby.

To prevent this from happening any alert Menkabong home

owner would take two pairs of water buffalo horns or, lacking
these, wooden slats. All village homes had openings at both roof
ends where cooking smoke could exit, and everyone knew it was
precisely these openings the Balang Balang preferred to use. For
this reason home owners would insert two crossed buffalo horns
or slats in these openings. Should the Balang Balang attempt to
enter a home it would quickly get its entrails entangled in the
crossed device, so being prevented from entering. Most homes in
the village had such horns or slats in place.

As usual, dusk had come suddenly, quickly. Glad to be home
before dark Yahaya tied his small boat to the ladder that extended
from the flats to his house. The tide was out, and he had to climb
a long way up to his home.

In their large group-owned, colorfully painted fishing boat
he and his two fishing partners had already put in a full day's
work. They hadn't caught much, but had some good laughs. Like
Yahaya, his buddies were former Buddhists turned Christians,
and they with their families attended the same church in Kota
Kinabalu as Yahaya and his wife did.

Still, chagrined not having caught anything worthwhile to
take home, Yahaya had gone out by himself in his own small boat
to try his luck for an hour or so. Trolling in midwater he had used
live squid, and had caught a five-pound Cobia. The fish had given
him a good fight, and that had been the enjoyable part of it. Although the Cobia was a fish prized by tourists and other visitors,
Yahaya himself didn't much like the meat of the fish. Still, it was
better than nothing.

Feeling unusually tired Yahaya reached the top of the ladder,
and went in. Planning to clean it later he laid the fish on the floor
beside the door. Slowly he found his way to a screened corner of
the room where he passed his water. As usual of late the simple
activity hurt. The stream burned, and with a groan he cramped
over. Lily, his wife, sat on a pillow in the middle of the room nursing Faizah, their three-month old baby. She looked at him with

concern. His discomfort when urinating certainly seemed to be getting worse.

Yahaya's problems with voiding his bladder had begun after his accident, fourteen years earlier. One afternoon he had been riding his motorized bike up to Kota Kinabalu, the large town a few kilometers north of his village. Suddenly his front wheel had caught in a crack in the asphalt. He had fallen, and although a passing minibus swerved trying to avoid hitting him, the wheels of it had run over his abdomen.

At the time his bladder had been full, and due to the impact it had been severed from the urethra. An ambulance had transported him to the hospital in KK, where doctors had spent hours repairing the damage. After a six-week stay he had come home again, but after a time strictures had begun to form at the surgery site. Because these were located right at the neck of the bladder Yahaya began to experience difficulties with urination.

Slowly he walked over to Lily and the baby, kissing both. Lily transferred the baby to her sling, and retrieved the Bible from the small table beside her. They regularly took turns reading out loud a chapter or two, discussing the contents afterwards. Today was Yahaya's turn, but just after he finished he doubled over with a sharp pain in his lower abdomen. Alarmed she went to him, and put her arms around his shoulders to comfort him. With a softly spoken *terimah kasih* he gave her a tiny hug back, then slowly got up and went to the phone; he knew something was seriously wrong. He called the clinic and left a message with a request for a morning appointment with the family doctor.

The next day their family physician examined him, but did not come to any conclusion. Instead, and after some discussion about what his problem might be, he referred him to a specialist in urological medicine. That appointment happened some two weeks later, and upon examining Yahaya the urologist felt that further testing needed be done. In the weeks that followed Yahaya was prodded and poked, and underwent a battery of tests, scans and screenings. Upon completion of them the urologist asked both Yahaya and his wife to come by the office. It was here the specialist informed them that Yahaya's pain and discomfort were not caused by the stricture, but by a cancer of the prostate that had metastasized into the pubic bone and other bones of the pelvis. It was with deep regret the urologist informed Yahaya that by a rough estimate he was given six months to live.

Once back home again Yahaya felt as though his life had already ended. Lily and he had been so happy with the beautiful little girl the Lord had given them. Now, without warning, all Yahaya's hopes of seeing her grow up, marry, and later for him to be able to play with his grandchildren, were cruelly dashed. His life was going to be cut short – he was going to die. He sat on the mat, and felt utterly tired, devoid of all energy, like a balloon with the air let out. Despair overcame him, and he let out a loud wail of anguish. Faizah began to cry. A deeply worried Lily, startled, picked her up, and looked at her husband with deep concern in her eyes. Then Yahaya sat quietly again.

Suddenly, out of hopelessness, there bubbled up a surge of red-hot anger, and he exploded. Picking up a jar he wildly threw it across the room, followed by a pewter vase. But when he grabbed hold of their cast-iron *wok* Lily grabbed him by the arm and stopped him. However, with his other hand he was able to grab hold of their family Bible, and slung it away from him as if it were a hot, poisonous item.

Faizah cried again. Yahaya stopped and looked at Lily who now also was softly crying. Yet, well aware of what he had just done, he somehow felt good about it. He was calm now, and once more in control of his emotions Yahaya began to reason with himself. He wondered how all this had come about. The accident itself had not have caused the cancer; that much he now knew. So if not from the accident, where had the cancer come from?

His mind went back to when his health problems had started, fourteen years ago. After the accident, he knew, he had never been the same; with the forming of strictures and scar tissue he always had to struggle with urinary problems. It was nothing short of a miracle he still had been able to sire a child. What else happened back then? His eyes widened as he suddenly realized what other life-changing event had taken place around that time: he had renounced Buddhism and become a Christian! Was that perhaps the connection he was looking for? It just had to be!

He shared his thoughts with Lily; Faisah had fallen asleep during nursing. Lily, too, was deeply distraught about the urologist's pronouncement. When Yahaya discussed his thoughts with her she could not help but allow for the possibility that he was right: that the cancer was a result of them having left the faith of their ancestors.

After a long discussion they agreed that next week, just once, perhaps, they should go back to their old Buddhist temple nearby, their old, familiar ancient temple, with all the plants growing in the eaves. There, they once again would throw their selected pieces of driftwood on the floor to determine yin-yang and, if that looked good, from the wall container pick up one of the numbered sticks to read the corresponding prayer, and burn paper money as a symbolic sacrifice.

Yahaya stood up, and went to get the beautiful hand-carved wooden box in which he kept important papers, including those having to do with the Sabah Protestant church of which both he and Lily were members. From the box he retrieved an old church bulletin, together with the W.C.C. form and envelope. Although there had been no previous desire to do this, they now filled in the form, and sealed it in the envelope. Together with Lily who carried the baby in the sling, they walked up to the mailbox beside the village store and mailed the letter. On a post nearby a *tokkeh*, the large blue lizard of the Far East, loudly screeched its approval. Yahaya lit a cigarette, and peacefully both he and Lily walked back the little distance to their home, making sure not to stumble over the water pipe. It had been a long day.

CHAPTER 15

Ivalu

It was late summer, and already now occasionally small ice floes clicked against the boat. The paddle barely rippled the surface as it smoothly slid into the cold waters of Frobisher Bay, and with a barely perceptible undulating movement the kayak steadily glided forward. Getting closer to shore Ivalu paddled slowly, keeping her eyes peeled for anything out of the ordinary. She loved this, and often went to the bay for a paddle just to unwind from the day's work in the small Iqaluit bakery. Iqaluit was the capital of Nunavut territory. It was located on Baffin Island, the largest of the islands in the northern Canadian archipelago.

The products she sold in the bakery were well above average in quality, but sometimes customers could be demanding, occasionally even unreasonable. Again today, after work, she had been especially tired, and so decided to unwind by going for her favorite mind-calming exercise. She could do this knowing that at least for the next couple of hours Aariak was being kept busy in the Nunavut Research Institute. Aariak, aged fifteen, was her problem child.

Although Ivalu had known about the disastrous impact alcohol could have especially on a developing fetus, at the early stages of her pregnancy it had not registered as something that also pertained to her. During her first trimester she even sometimes lapsed into binge-drinking, and it was only later in her pregnancy she had begun to be concerned about it, and had sought help. But by then the harm had been done. In the fetus the devastating effects of F.A.S.D., Fetal Alcohol Spectrum Disorder, were already in the making, later to give rise to the dreaded fetal alcohol syndrome with its attendant social problems and learning difficulties. Because at birth Aariak's first bowel movement, the meconium, had not been checked for the presence of ethyl esters, for a long time her F.A.S.D. condition had remained undiagnosed.

In the early years Aariak had been a docile child, who seldom cried. Right from Kindergarten she had shown to be good in art, and generally did passably well in school. Unfortunately, she had liked socializing far better than completing homework. However, it was during her pre-adolescent years that problems first began to emerge. Aariak had a sweet tooth, and often pilfered candies and other sweets from her classmates at school. She also began to pick for friends children who were not a good influence on her.

By now Ivalu had begun to have a good idea what kind of difficulties Aariak would likely have to face later in life. Becoming increasingly concerned, and for some guidance in the matter, she had gone to Father Brown, the rector of the Iqaluit Anglican Church. She did not attend his church, did not attend any church, but the priest had taken courses in counseling, conflict resolution and mediation. He was a wise man, and had been of help to many. In Ivalu's case, too, he had made several common sense suggestions, suggestions she had implemented, and that had seemed to help for a while. But only for a while.

The wind picked up. She leaned into the coaming and with several strong forward sweep strokes turned the kayak around, her spray skirt getting soaked by the whipped-up waves. She took off her mitt and placed her hand in the water – it was cold. There was little current here, but she now faced a strong wind, and had to work much harder. Feathering her paddle she headed for the wharf, another half hour away.

Staying close to shore she passed large masses of shiny, black rock. She knew that these were the kinds of rocks that contained the gold-gleaming pyrites. She also knew that some five centuries earlier Frobisher, in the mistaken notion they contained gold, had taken two hundred tons of these rocks to England and narrowly escaped being thrown in jail for his efforts. Tough beans, she thought. Contentedly, but getting a little tired, she stopped for a spell, and let the kayak slowly drift back a little ways.

The wind pushed the boat towards the shore, and with her one hand she hung on to a crinkly kelp leaf, stopping the drift. Already many weeks ago the hummocky wetlands to her right had begun to turn brown, and now they looked barren, cold, and inhospitable. The tundra blossoms had gone, and it wouldn't be long before the first snow would fall and the bay would become first choked with ice floes and then solidly frozen over. What made it happen every year?

She reflected on the Creator who annually wielded his magic wand turning water into ice and then into water again, eggs into birds, buds into flowers, and the long darkness into a burst of sunshine. Why couldn't he or she work that kind of magic on Aariak?

Overhead a hungry gyrfalcon screeched briefly and swooped down to what likely was a char, or whitefish. The bird missed, and flew off over the bay to her left. Just past Katannilik Park she got out of the kayak and waded to shore, dragging the boat behind her. Once there she up-turned it, placing the paddle and pump underneath. Walking the short distance to her home she rinsed her cold legs and feet in a bucket of luscious warm water, changed clothes, and sat down. She turned up the electric heat and, tired from her paddle, dozed off.

She was awakened by Aariak who came in through the back door, humming. The girl was an hour earlier than usual and together with her humming this was unusual. Ivalu immediately suspected something wasn't quite right, but decided not to say anything. Aariak went up to her room. Some ten minutes later the videophone flashed. She picked it up, and it was then that Equeesik, the director of the Research Institute, told her that Aariak had been sent home because of a major infraction of one of the Institute rules: once again she had been doing drugs. Ivalu thanked Equeesik for the information, and promised to deal with the matter forthwith.

Ivalu sighed deeply, and sat down. It seemed there was no end to Aariak's substance abuse, and the conversation with Equeesik had drained her. Two weeks earlier the same thing had happened. At the time there had been a deeply serious discussion with both Equeesik and Father Brown present. Following that meeting Ivalu had informed Aariak that should it happen again truly grave consequences would have to be faced: in no uncertain terms Ivalu told her that should it happen only once more she would have to leave home for treatment, likely off island.

By all concerned it was hoped that Aariak would turn a new leaf. However, today it had become clear this really had not happened, and the consequence of her behavior had to be faced. Within the week the arrangements were finalized: for treatment she was going to be sent to the substance abuse department of the Janeway Health and Rehabilitation Centre in St. John's, Newfoundland.

Ivalu had hoped Aariak would give some indication of feeling badly about her behavior. However, as on so many occasions before, this was not to be. Aariak acted as if she would actually be glad to be away from Iqaluit, and away from her Mom: Hey, a little adventure!

Ivalu was much saddened about the way her daughter was acting. It was of deep concern to her not so much because the girl made wrong decisions for, she thought, everybody occasionally does that. What troubled her more than anything was that Aariak never ever gave evidence of feeling sorry about her wrong-doings. In addition to never giving any thought to consequences of any of her actions, the girl simply had no innate sense of remorse. To Ivalu it was not so much what the girl did, as what she did *not* do.

When it was Aariak's time to leave she did not in any way appear to be vexed or disturbed. Ivalu herself brought her to the airport. Looking forward to her plane trip Aariak simply left with a wave of her hand and a happy "Bye Mom!" as if nothing had happened, as if she just left for school. Walking briskly she went through the boarding gate. Then, without looking back, she rounded a partition, and was gone from sight.

Ivalu went home. Tonight a staff pot-luck supper was going to be held in the family room above the bakery. The employees got together like this every other month or so, and usually that was a lot of fun. But with all that had happened today she really didn't feel much like going. Still, she went to the bedroom to put on her favorite bright red dress thinking it might lift her mood. She walked up to the dresser and opened the drawer to take out her wallet, and started: it wasn't there! She hadn't by accident put it in her purse, had she?

Retrieving her purse from behind its secret place underneath the recliner she opened it, but it wasn't there either. Where could it be? Who could have . . . Her head jerked up as suddenly it dawned on her: only Aariak could have done this. Only Aariak knew where her purse was, and only Aariak had had the opportunity! Defeated, she sat in her chair and broke down.

Ivalu cried for a long time, but then got up, washed her face, and made tea. Slowly her sadness gave away to anger. What was the matter with this girl? And what was the matter with the Creator? Why did he, or she, or whatever, just sit there in the cold sky watching with a cold heart all these happenings in this cold land? Did he only involve himself with the things that *he* liked to do like making the world cold and dark in winter and warm and pretty in summer? Did he not involve himself at all in her personal life?

Giving in to a sudden thought she went to her bookcase and from a small stack of papers retrieved one of the flyers that had come with the paper some days ago. It had a large brown envelope with it, and a questionnaire that had to be filled in and mailed to an organization called the W.C.C. She had glanced at it, and had understood it had to do with complaints people had about the actions of the Creator. Well, fancy that: she was just in the right mood for that. She hadn't read it yet, and so opened it and read the contents. After filling in the form she put on her mukluks, went to the car, and unplugged the block heater. On her way to the potluck she stopped by the post-office and unhesitatingly mailed the letter.

CHAPTER 16

Sitti

"*Holong rohanku di ho!*" Pandingkar cried out to Sitti, "I love you!" But Sitti said nothing in return, and turned away from him. She walked up to the village centre and sat down in one of the stone chairs under the large Waringin tree. He followed her, and kept talking: "I promise you, I'll never drink again," then added nonsensically, "If I do I'll kill myself." But Sitti stood up, and once again turned away from him. She walked up to her jabu, her home near the end of the street that divided the two sections of the Karo Batak *huta*, the village on Samosir Island, where she lived.

Like all the others in the street, her home was built on poles. Constructed of *pekki* wood, all parts of it were fastened with rope from the *ijuk* palm, and wooden pins. The thatched, narrow roof rose up steeply at both ends and culminated in two beautifully carved and painted sharp points. Colorfully decorated, the home contrasted sharply with the various greens of the jungle edge just beyond. Sitti loved her home; it had been her home for all fifteen years of her life. Grasping the longer of the two bamboo poles that formed the basic structure of the ladder Sitti quickly climbed up and disappeared into the small opening, bending low as she went in. Pandingkar, who had followed from a distance, stood forlornly in the street below. Sitti turned around, and as she put her head back into the opening she yelled at him, "I don't ever want to see you again, I hate you!"

The Batak people live in a small area on the Northern tip of Sumatra, one of the larger islands that make up the Indonesian archipelago. They mostly inhabit the hill country around Lake Toba, a large mountain lake in the interior. Samosir, an island in the lake, is also home to many Bataks, and was the island where Sitti and Pandankar lived. On Samosir nearly all Bataks were from the Karo clan. Most of them were Christians who had built a church there. Pandankar had found employment in the hotel industry around the island, had made a good life for himself, and when he had met Sitti his joy had seemed complete.

Sitti was the oldest daughter of Adji Panurat. Her mother had died at the birth of her younger sibling, Taring, who was away visiting a friend in a nearby village. Her friendship with Pandingkar, who was from a different Batak clan, had brought Sitti plenty of joy in her life. She really liked him, loved him, even. He was handsome, and funny, and also very romantic, often bringing her bouquets of flowers from the jungle. But Pandingkar had a huge problem: he was an alcoholic, and Sitti and he had had this kind of fight many times before.

Pandingkar had found work as a waiter and bartender in a tourist hotel by the lake. In this position he often had to serve Arak, a strong spirit favored by tourists, a drink also Pandingkar had begun to like. Sitti had never seen anything wrong with consuming an alcoholic beverage now and then, but usually this had consisted of a Bintang or some other beer. Arak was different. Arak, distilled from black rice and coconut milk, rendered a colorless, sugarless spirit with high alcohol content. Pandankar had become addicted to it, and at the young age of twenty-one he had become an alcoholic.

Inside her home Sitti sat on the woven mat that covered a large part of the floor, and cried. Why had God allowed Pandingkar to come into her life? Why had he allowed him to become an alcoholic? Last night they had gone to a performance of a wonderful *wayang* play performed by a Javanese artist group. True, wayang was a Hindu shadow play whereas she was a Christian, but the performance of such a play was quite a cultural event, and almost everyone on the island had gone. As on several other occasions Pandingkar had already been partying by himself before he picked her up, and after the play it was no doubt his semi-inebriated state that had contributed hugely to the fight he had gotten into with another man. It had been an ugly scene, and Sitti had gone home alone, crying.

She looked through one of the many small openings in the wall of her home and saw that Pandingkar was still there. He sat on his haunches, his arms resting on his knees in the typical Batak resting position. He looked small, and vulnerable, and she couldn't help but feel sorry for him. He mostly was such a nice, gentle guy. If only the Arak hadn't come between them. Still, it wasn't very long before she went outside again to talk to him.

They went for a long walk along the bamboo hedge that surrounded the entire huta, and before long the fighting episode of the night before was put behind them. He told her repeatedly that he truly loved her, and that he would not ever touch Arak again. In the end she just had to believe him: he was too serious and remorseful not to really have meant what he said. And then their talk drifted into wedding plans again. They both had discussed this many times before, but only in a tentative way. Now, for the first time, they had a truly serious talk about it, and also for the first time they felt marriage was within the realm of possibility. However, Pandingkar then informed her that unless they would marry soon there was a possibility they would have to wait a little while.

During their walk he had told her he had become involved with the Aceh Sumatra National Liberation Front, an organization that sought to "liberate" Sumatra from the Indonesian "suppression," and to make it a sovereign nation. The movement had really grown after a perceived lack of adequate relief effort by Indonesian authorities after the cataclysmic Boxing Day Tsunami some fifty-odd years ago. She knew about the movement, for her father had spoken to her about it on several occasions, had in fact sympathized with it. Pandingkar spoke passionately about it, and actually got Sitti quite interested.

One thing she did not like, though, was that many of those involved were required to undergo specialized military training in Libya. For although Libya no longer had the reputation of the terrorist country it had been under strong man President Mumar al-Khadafi, it still often clandestinely provided opportunity for terrorist organizations to train on Libyan soil. As he would become more involved with the movement, he told Sitti, at some time in the future he, too, would have to go there for specialized training.

A few days later Sitti and Pandankar discussed the wedding with their respective parents: Sitti with her father and Pandingkar with his parents. To the young couple's delight both sides agreed the wedding could go ahead, and would take place as soon as details could be arranged. A mutually agreed upon wedding date was set for later that month.

It was early morning of the wedding day. A brief tropical rainfall had washed away all dust off shrubbery and trees, and already the sun was hot, with clouds of steam rising everywhere. Well over four hundred guests from all over the island had gathered in the central square, where under a large canvas awning mounds of food were being prepared. Music blared from several strategically placed speakers, and before long, under tumultuous clapping of hands, the bride and groom appeared. They were dressed in a mix of traditional Karo and Western clothing and decked out in gold jewelry: the typical Karo Batak wedding ceremony could now officially begin.

First the dowry was paid, for no celebration could commence until that was completed to the satisfaction of both parties. Then the gifts were brought on, and as usual everybody was nosy about which guests brought what. As always one of the most important gifts was bedding for the nuptial bed, but the weightiest present of all was still the gift of a live hen, the symbol of fertility. Under much laughter and jokes all gifts were gratefully accepted, and the feast began.

There was plenty of everything, from *nasi padang* to vegetables and fruit, from chicken to *bahmi goreng*, all of it eaten by hand and washed away with plenty of beer. Afterwards followed both traditional and western dancing, accompanied by the ever-present guitars seemingly every Batak knew how to play. In time the festivities drew to a close, leftovers were taken home, and everything was cleaned up. And so it all ended: Pandingkar and Sitti were married.

About four months after the wedding Pandingkar came home drunk for the first time. There was a big scene, and especially with Sitti now being pregnant it was a deeply traumatic experience. Over the weeks and months that followed this happened more and more often. Pandingkar had become totally disinterested in religion; nearly always now Sitti would have to go to church by herself. Oddly, her father seemed to side with Pandingkar, and told her not to take matters so seriously. Sitti, however, felt betrayed. When Pandingkar came home drunk one more time she told him to stay out and sleep somewhere else. He ranted and raved, but Sitti did not let him in. That night Pandingkar slept outside in the square.

Sitti lay on her mat inside her home, tossing and turning, not being able to sleep. She thought about her life, the disappointment Pandingkar had brought her, and what future she had with him and the life that was growing inside her. She began to sob. What must she do? How could she possibly face a life with a baby and with a husband who was a drunk? Perhaps she should move away, off island, but where would she go?

She sat up. After drying her face she lit the small lamp that hung suspended from the crossbeam above her. Seeing her old New Testament lying in the corner she picked it up, and opened it. The first thing her eyes fell on was the well-known passage in Philippians, "Rejoice in the Lord always. I will say it again: Rejoice!"

It was too much. In a sudden spurt of anger she took the New Testament and hurled it out the door opening into the dark night. There. Let Pandingkar read it. Let the dogs read it. She hated Pandingkar! And she hated God! Suddenly she thought of something else.

On hands and knees she crawled around in the scant light of the lamp and found the brown envelope she was looking for lying on the floor next to the sleeping area. She knew about the W.C.C. questionnaire, because some weeks back she and father had discussed it. Like Pandingkar, he seldom went to church anymore, and wouldn't mind one bit if she used the form – might like it, even. Next morning she filled it in, enclosed it in the envelope, and brought it to the island's only bookstore, the *toko buku*. There, she gave the envelope to the owner who once a month took all island mail to the main post-office in Medan. Sitti saw him place the envelope in a large leather pouch, and with a happy *selamat tinggal* she left for home.

CHAPTER 17

Louis and Andrée

It was late afternoon, and getting dark. Louis Cadotte stood on the large sundeck at the front of his house in Houston, a small town approximately halfway up the beautiful Canadian coastal province of British Columbia. The deck had a thin cover of snow, and where the early morning sun had begun to thaw it into wet patches the cold of the late afternoon had already frozen them dry. He listened to the hiss of truck tires as massive transport vehicles whizzed by on the old Yellowhead, Highway 16, the widened and re-surfaced expressway that had been completed only three years earlier.

A worthy and necessary addition to the Northern railroad system the Highway stretched from Edmonton in the province of Alberta through the Yellowhead Pass in the Rockies to Prince George, an original British Columbia mill town that over the years had become the hub of the north, a cosmopolitan mega city. From there the expressway ran through Vanderhoof, Smithers and Terrace to Prince Rupert, the large coastal city with its refurbished harbor and newly constructed grain elevators. Louis was familiar with the route.

A former driver with Allied Truck Lines he had driven the road many times, had especially taken much pleasure from the ever-changing scenery of the passing seasons. He and his family had lived in Burns Lake, a small town east of Houston. But when Louis had been offered a lucrative snowmobile franchise in Houston, a small sawmill town about eighty kilometers farther west, he had quit his truck-driver's job and he his family had moved to Houston and bought a home there.

The Cadottes had two boys, Charlie and Billy. At nineteen, Charlie was the elder of the two. Billy, sixteen, had been a student in grade eleven at the brand new *Claude Parish* Public Secondary School. Opened five years earlier the school, renamed after Houston's dynamic first mayor, was renowned for its utterly modern computer facilities and miniature sports complex. It hugely benefited all local and area students, and the brand-new facility had begun to draw them from as far away as Topley and Telkwa.

As all mothers do, Andrée regularly compared the growth pattern of her own baby with those of her friends' babies. When at about the age of eight months Charlie had seemed "floppy" and had neither begun to crawl nor shown any interest in supporting himself or pulling himself up, he had become of some concern to the Cadottes. Their family doctor, like the parents, had also become concerned about the baby's development, and grew more so when it became evident that when compared with other babies of the same age Charlie's vocalizations, too, seemed underdeveloped. For these reasons the doctor had referred the child to a pediatrician in Prince George, and it was there that Charlie was diagnosed as a C.P., a cerebral palsied child.

When a shocked Louis and Andrée inquired how that could have come about the specialist opined that either before or during his birth, Charlie had likely suffered oxygen deprivation to the brain, and it was this that had resulted in a permanent disruption between that organ and his muscular system.

Charlie's growing up years had been challenging to his parents. Once in high school Charlie had been fully accepted, and had been one of the crowd. He was popular, and always went along on typical high school outings and parties: high school had been a very inclusive experience for him. But this had not been the case in grade school.

Early on Charlie's spasticity and spells of loud laughter had set him apart from the other children. Because of this, especially in the earlier grades, some of the children had regarded him not only as "different," but weird, and simply had not accepted him as one of theirs. Although there were also those children who were deeply sensitive, kind and helpful to him, he sometimes was so cruelly hurt by the comments and gibes of those who were not that there had been times he no longer wanted to go back to school.

The matter became even more complicated when because the way Charlie acted several of the kids became scared of him, which resulted in some parents objecting to his presence in the same room with their own children. Subsequent consultations with principal and staff improved these misgivings somewhat. However, because of this business several of these parents had become at odds with the Cadottes, and to Charlie's parents the experiences of the early years had been unsettling and difficult ones. Charlie, in spite of his handicap, was a bright child, and appeared to remain unaffected by it all. He seemed to roll through the controversy he unwittingly had caused better and more smoothly than many of the adults.

With Billy it was an entirely different situation. Billy was of just average intelligence, but had assets that made a great difference in his life: from day one Billy had been a most attractive looking child with a pleasant and happy disposition, both of which had characterized his all too brief life. Early on children had flocked to him like bees to a particularly pleasing spring flower. They wanted to play with him, and be his friend. Fortunately, Billy's personality, even when young, enabled him to handle the attention he received with a measure of aplomb and equanimity.

Billy was a child who was easy to love, and his growing up years were characterized by joy and laughter. At the age of fifteen, already six feet, he cut a striking figure: broad shouldered, with dark, curly locks, deep brown eyes and a ready and infectious laugh. He had no difficulty attracting appreciative glances from the girls, his own age as well as older ones, both in school and outside of it.

He and Charlie had a good relationship. The boys were fond of each other, and hung around together a lot. One morning, when with their parents on a shopping trip to Smithers, a town 40 km west of Houston, they had observed in the display window of one of the two motor bicycle shops in town a beautiful-looking second-hand bike. It was an older *KRISS 100*, a 100cc bike made by the MODENAS Corporation in Malaysia. Billy immediately imagined himself riding the bike with Charlie on the rear seat. They both became incredibly excited about the idea of having a bike like that, and begun sweet-talking Louis and Andreé to please pretty please buy it for them.

After initial hesitation – after all, Billy was only fifteen – they gave in, and a week later, a sunny late-winter afternoon, they went to Smithers with the pickup and bought the bike, planning to purchase some accessories in the weeks to come.

The boys were overjoyed. The following week Billy got his first riding lessons, with Louis the capable instructor. Billy did well, and picked up the basics fast. At first he just rode along the length of the driveway, and then learned to circle around by the edge of the road and to ride back. It wasn't long before Louis felt comfortable enough to tell Billy he thought him ready for a first real ride. They would go to Morrice River Road, a few kilometers west of town, where Billy would ride the bike, and Louis with Charlie would ride behind him in the pickup.

Morrice River Road ran alongside the river of the same name, a body of water favored by anglers looking for Spring Salmon and Chinook. Around three o'clock on a Thursday afternoon Billy had run home from school – Louis and Charlie were already waiting. As it would begin to darken soon, the threesome had to hurry up, so off they went.

Both bike and pickup were traveling at a leisurely twenty-five kilometers per hour, well below the speed limit, when a curve to the right loomed ahead. Louis saw Billy beginning to take oncoming curve too far to the left and in alarm honked his horn to warn him. It was too late. Because of the particularly loud engine of the *KRISS* neither Billy, nor Louis and Charlie in the cabin of the pickup, had heard the logging truck coming full tilt around the curve. The head-on collision shattered the bike, parts of it thrown with great force into the bushes on the side of the road. Billy was thrown clear, landing into the shoulder on the opposite site right at the edge of the river. He was killed instantly.

Louis and Andreé had walked up to the Bulkley, the river a block east of their home on North Copeland Avenue. Charlie had remained home playing a video game. It was cold and getting dark. The streetlight at the end of Fifth Street cast an unearthly glow on the river ice in front of them where a thin layer of snow revealed crisscrossed tracks of children, dogs and moose, and pockmarked, broken blisters of frozen old snow hid the masses of black, cold water swirling beneath them. Before long the river would shed her frosty smile in exchange for a total, final spasm of roaring laughter, and release her struggling, churning load into the already distended form of her big sister, the Skeena. Soon, now, its wild waters would rush past borders sunk low in antici-pation and accommodation of a river gone wild: Spring break-up.

It was three weeks after the terrible accident. The news of Billy's death had sent shockwaves throughout the entire North Country. From as far away as Prince George and Rupert, many, especially teenagers, had known Billy. The loss was felt especially keenly at the school, and grief counselors had come to help the students through the difficult time of coping with the loss of their friend.

Louis and Andreé held hands as they slowly walked back home. When they got into the door they were greeted by their minister who had driven up during their absence and had been let in by Charlie. The Reverend Taekema was the preacher at the Community Church in Smithers, the church they attended. He was a truly sincere man, and had tried very hard to help the

Cadottes deal with their grief. But their sadness was deep, and instead of lessening, their feelings of despair at the pit of their stomachs seemed to intensify as the weeks had gone by.

On impulse, a week after that last visit, Louis pulled out the large brown envelope from underneath a stack of papers with in it the W.C.C. questionnaire. He read again the information it contained. For some time he and Andreé discussed it, then came to an agreement. They filled it in and together next morning they walked to the post office downtown, and placed it in the mailbox.

CHAPTER 18

W.C.C. Head Office

The sorting room in the W.C.C. head office in Geneva was nearly empty. Still suddenly, with a heartfelt "Hallelujah," the last worker pushed back her chair and looked at the final, small stack of forms: twelve in all. The shredders had just quit humming, and after many months of work everything was suddenly quiet. It felt decidedly strange.

Gurpreet Cheema, the head collator, took the remaining twelve forms and placed them gently, almost reverentially, in a leather attaché case. He thanked his co-workers for their hard work over the past two years, and although it was still early afternoon gave them the rest of the day off. Walking down the hall he took the elevator to the third floor, exited, and took the few steps to the board room. Here, the General Secretaries had gathered, including Klaas Blik, who the day before officially had been voted in as Pieter Retief's permanent replacement as General Secretary for all of Africa. Gurpreet knocked, and was let in by Maria Sanchez. On behalf of the Secretaries she thanked him for all the work he and his helpers had done, and accepted the attaché case from him. He left, softly closing the door behind him.

Maria Sanchez turned to the Secretaries and looked at them thoughtfully. Not saying anything she laid the attaché case on the table, opened it, and took out the completed forms. She walked up to the projection table and inserted then forms. Upon the push of a button two things happened simultaneously: the sec-

92

tions of the wall at the end of the room slid open to reveal a large screen, and the room darkened. Almost immediately all pertinent information regarding the first complainant, Geertje, together with her stated reasons for being angry with God, began to scroll down.

Everyone read along, transfixed. As the readings progressed they became in a personal way familiar with the hurts of God's people across the globe, and shortly any troubles or discomforts they themselves had experienced seemed to pale in comparison. When it all was finished they had become still, and for a long while contemplated what they had just seen and heard. After a while Maria Sanchez called for round prayer, and in turn all gave voice to the sorrow that was felt in his or her own heart. Moved with compassion, they asked for guidance from above as they prayed for a long, long time.

In the discussion and evaluation that followed it was noted that, as ordered, the selection committee had ended up with twelve serious accusations and criticisms of God, and that the complaints had come from all over the planet. Furthermore, with five females, five males, and two couples, the Secretaries felt there was an excellent gender representation. They also thought Gurpreet and his helpers had done an amazing job with the final selection from the hundreds of thousands of submissions, and they unanimously agreed to present both him and his helpers with specially-made commemorative plaques.

After a while the delegates seated themselves alongside another table, right by one of the windows from which they could see the towering stream of water from the newly re-constructed, high-spouting Jet d'Eau fountain in the lake. Following some final discussions they had Communion together, and shortly thereafter said their good-byes and made arrangements to go back to their own home and country.

CHAPTER 19

The 20th W.C.C. General Assembly, AD 2061, May 20

A t the time of its invention the vid-byte bandwidth that was going to be used at the Assembly had been a technological breakthrough, and via the digital pathway on the three-dimensional liquid-crystal display screen the writing was incredibly clear. The large hall in the W.C.C. head office in Geneva was packed, for it was here the momentous communication with God was scheduled to occur. Everyone was wound tighter than a drumhead. Would God actually *directly* communicate with them as he had done in the Old Testament?

A loud buzz filled the hall as well over a thousand delegates from all over the world met up with old friends and discussed the happenings of the past two years. Suddenly the gigantic video screen in the front lit up. All turned in their seats to face it, and fell silent. Awestruck, and with great anticipation they looked at it, wondering what was going to happen. Still suddenly, in Imanto, the screen began to fill with writing:

Dear Children,
I am deeply, deeply saddened about your hurts,
your anguish,

and your sorrows.
It is not what I had wanted for you.

In the beginning it all was so good.
There was peace,
and Shalom,
and there was neither harm
- nor destruction
in all my holy mountain.

It was a time when the wolf and the lamb fed together,
and the lion ate straw like the ox,
a time when I answered people before I was called
and heard them while they were still speaking.

But then, as you know,
all that changed when sin came into the world.

———

And now, Geertje, you are my first complainant.
You ask where I was
in your need.

You ask
what happened to my oft-proclaimed faithfulness,
and wonder
why I allowed your marriage to go
"on the rocks."

Believe me, Geertje, it is not what I wanted to happen for you,
for remember, Geertje,
I am love,
and love doesn't want to hurt.

Therefore, Geertje, believe in me.
Trust in me.
For I can bring solace,
and somehow,

beyond your understanding,
I can make all things well.

Come, Geertje,
come talk with me.

Sadiq, I am so deeply saddened about your plight.

First you lost your beloved parents,
and then the use of your legs.
It is almost understandable that you question my existence!

But, Sadiq, if I would not exist,
what could possibly be the answer to your question
how a butterfly can come out of a cocoon,
and a particular color flower out of an Acacia tree?

The answer, dear Sadiq, is that such miracles
can only be performed through my divine design.

Sadiq, I exist.
I am.
And if you let it,
my Spirit will bear witness to that in your heart.

Trust me, Sadiq.
Trust in my love.
Trust me to be a comfort to you.

Come, Sadiq,
come talk with me.

Dear Sook,
How I grieved with you
when you lost your dear Hyun-Ki,
the love of your life.

The two of you loved me so,
dedicated your lives to me,
and then the unthinkable happened.
Dear child,
I know how you grieve.

But if you would open the Scriptures,
even today,
you will hear me speak to you
in special ways.

For I am still the Great Comforter
who can dry all tears,
and bring solace,
the kind of solace that will heal you,
quiet your spirit,
and again gladden your heart.

Dear Sook,
I miss you.
Please open my Word, Sook,
and read it.

Come,
trust me,
and talk with me.

Dear Derek,
Dear, sorrowing Derek,
I wept with you
when you lost your wife,
and I wept with you
when you lost your boys.

I did not want those things to happen, Derek.
There is so much sadness, and hurt, and pain, and brokenness in the
world. But, Derek, it still is my world!
I know what a difficult time this is for you,

but I so very much miss your talking to me.
I want to console you,
hold your hand again, Derek,
walk with you,
and send my angels to bear you up.

Derek,
I know you are my disciple.
I know that in spite of your sadness
you still love me.
Therefore I can still bring you
the peace that passes all understanding,
and misunderstanding.

Dear Derek,
let me weep with you,
let me sorrow with you,
let us shed our tears together.

Derek, come,
come talk with me.

Dear Pedro,
dear Padre Pedro,
dear friend of mine.

What a difficult time you had,
and what a tough decision you had to make.

But in the end, Pedro,
you made a decision
that made me love you all the more.

This was not because you chose to continue serving me "full-time,"
for many do that,
be they bakers,
plumbers,
or computer software designers.

I love you all the more
because you chose to be true to your vow,
and for you,
dear friend,
that was the right choice.

In the years ahead, Pedro,
I shall be with both you,
and Althea,
in special ways.

Keep trusting in me, Pedro,
for all things will work together for good.

Dear Pedro,
please, keep talking with me.

Dear Tala,

I miss you, Tala.
Come back to me!

You went to a healer to heal your body,
for you wanted your body to be whole.
Sadly, that did not happen.

But what could happen, Tala,
and even more important,
is the healing of your spirit.

Tala, because of my son Jesus' sacrifice on the cross,
a new, everlasting life
awaits all those who believe in him,
a new life, in a new body.
That is my promise to you.

Dear Tala,

come.
Trust me.
Talk with me.

Louisa, there is a problem in your life.
I know this has to do with the break-up of your relationship with a
girl.

I am aware this relationship was of the kind
normally expected to exist between a woman, and a man.
You yourself harbored questions about that relationship,
and struggled with the knowledge that your desire,
although not needing to be suppressed,
needed to be regulated within the confines of your faith commitment
to me.

You were confused, Louisa,
and began to wonder if I was just a name "somewhere up there,"
like a noun,
rather than an actively working entity,
like a verb.

Louisa, I am both.
I am like a "noun," for I am the NAME above all names,
and I am also like a "verb," for I am the WORD made flesh.

Louisa,
there was a time you regularly called upon my NAME,
and I was active in your life.
Some time ago you decided upon a Christian college for your
education.
That decision flowed from a sincere desire to serve me.

Louisa, re-visit that desire.
Think through the choices you made.
For like everyone else, you, too, are called to holiness.

Come, Louisa,

come,
trust me,
and talk with me.

Dear Wes and Sara.
I have not heard from you for a while,
and I miss you.

I know you feel guilty.

I know you feel sad.

But listen,
I have good news:

Feel guilty no longer,
for Jesus' blood has washed you whiter than snow.

And be sad no longer,
for your baby is with me,
and is now whole.

Dear Wes and Sara,
this is another day.

Come,
rejoice and be glad.

Come,
talk with me.

Dear Yahaya,

Because over the years you have faithfully read my Word,
you know
that any attempt to break free from suffering

*through personal effort
is doomed for failure.*

*You can not be your own savior, Yahaya.
You need an outside source.*

*Dear Yahaya,
you need
ME.*

*For I am your Savior.
I can bring you peace.
Dear Yahaya,
Come.
Talk with me.*

*Dear Ivalu,
here I am,
your Creator.*

I, too, am deeply saddened by the way things turned out.

*But, Ivalu,
healing is available for both you,
and Aariak:
there is still balm in Gilead.*

*When kayaking, just listen for my whispering voice
in the cries of the seagulls,
in the sough of the paddle,
and in the sounds of the waves as they gently lap the shore.*

*But, Ivalu, also in the stillness of the night.
And perhaps,
just maybe,
also during worship services in your little Iqaluit church.
Dear Ivalu,*

come,
trust me,
and talk with me.

Dear Sitti:

Rejoice!
I'll say it again: rejoice! For I have good news!
You say you hate me,
and to prove that you threw your New Testament out of your home.

But, dear Sitti:
although you threw my written Word out of your home
you could not throw the "Word-made-flesh" out of your heart!

Yes, dear Sitti, I am still there,
and I am there to stay.
For you are mine,
and I am yours.

And, Sitti,
although at this time everything seems dark,
once again the light of my love
will break through.
I promise you: I will heal,
and in a strange new way make everything alright.

Rejoice, Sitti!
I promise
you will have
"Joy in the morning!"

Come, girl, come.
Come,
talk with me.

Dear Louis and Andreé,

With you, I, too, weep about the loss of your son.
But yet you must be glad,
for Billy is now here, with me:
he stands with the white-robed multitude
in front of the Lamb.
He is fine.

Keep the faith, Louis and Andreé,
and keep trusting in me.
For then, someday, you will be here, too.
With me.
And with Billy.
Therefore do not mourn as those who have no hope.
Remember: I am the Great Comforter.
I can dry your tears
and turn your mourning into gladness.

Come.
Talk with me.

———

In conclusion:

Dear children,
I am aware
that sometimes you can not understand
why certain things
happened in your lives,
occurrences that don't make sense to you.

But remember,
to many events you can not apply human logic.
I am not subject to human logic,
for I am God.

Far more important,

even though this may not always be easy for you to see,
remember that

I am Love!

That love is sufficient to heal every hurt,
soothe every sorrow,
ease every pain,
and dry every tear.
And this well of my love never runs dry:
My Love Is Forever.

God

CHAPTER 20

Closing of the Conference

The screen went blank. People turned to each other in their chairs, and slowly the large hall began to fill with softly spoken voices. Here and there one got up to make use of the facilities, and another walked up to friends they had not seen for some time. Deeply, and at length, people began to discuss what they had witnessed. This went on for some time until the lunch buzzer sounded and everyone began to file out of the room into the eating area, where lunch had been prepared, and informal talks continued.

After lunch a final meeting was scheduled. It was chaired by Maria Sanchez who briefly recalled the proceedings of the last few days, culminating in God's Imanto address. Following this she requested everyone to rise, and closed with prayer and the apostolic blessing. But when everyone began to turn around ready to leave, she held up her hand, and one more time asked for attention.

"Dear friends," she said, "Many of you may know that on the occasion of installation of clergy in the Greek Orthodox Church it is common to 'send them off' with the congregational '*AXIOS*,' or 'He Is Worthy.' After what we have heard and seen this morning I now invite you all to praise our Lord in the same manner."

Everyone joined in, and many hands were raised in adoration as the '*AXIOS*' was intoned in unison, resounding through the hall for many minutes. There were few dry eyes amongst the delegates, but after a while slowly the chanting diminished and the hundreds of delegates began to exit.

Not everyone went immediately back to their hotel or other lodgings. It was still early afternoon, the sun was shining, and many, often in small groups, went to the heart of the old town to visit the "Cathedrale de St-Pierre," the church that had been the headquarters of the Reformation. Others walked along the "Promenade des Bastions" to the famed statuary wall and inscription that celebrated the great figures of the "orthodox" Reformation, John Calvin, Guillaume Farel, Theodore Beza and John Knox. But as everything must end the following day saw most delegates depart for their own country and home. The conference was over.

CHAPTER 21

Aftermath

The happenings in Geneva were reported in all the media. In a broken, groaning world, a world desperate for healing, God's messages of comfort and hope to the twelve complainants spread like wildfire, and across the globe countless of God's despairing, hurt, and grief-stricken children took God's letters to the twelve as also addressed to them, taking and applying them to their own hearts and lives.

And so the events of the 2061 W.C.C. Assembly brought new faith and a spirit of renewal and optimism to many a church and chapel. Countless people, some for the first time, others for the first time in a long while, experienced the ultimate, all-transcending peace of God.

CHAPTER 22

Bishop Karamios

After the morning service, Bishop Karamios had gone to his little office. He sat down in his old leather chair and sighed deeply. It had been an exhausting morning. Slowly he got up and went to the table where lay his old Bible. His eyes were tired, but his heart rejoiced.

After the message of this morning he had paused for a moment, and then had confessed to the members of his congregation that all his life he had struggled with alcoholism. Subsequently he had asked their forgiveness, and through his own tear-stained eyes he had seen that the expressions of his people were now no longer cold, no longer reflecting a silent loathing or revulsion. Instead he saw warmth, empathy, and an understanding that told him they had indeed forgiven him.

He opened his Bible to one of his favorite passages, that of chapter sixty-five of the prophet Isaiah:

"Behold, I will create new heavens and a new earth.
The former things will not be remembered,
nor will they come to mind...
The wolf and the lamb will feed together,
and the lion will eat straw like the ox...
They will neither harm nor destroy
in all my holy mountain..."

He lay his head on the passage. He was very, very tired, and almost asleep. He looked at an old icon reproduction of the Vladimir Madonna that hung beside his desk. On it the baby Jesus, who looked away in the distance, was held by his mother in the crook of her right arm. The baby slowly turned his head, looked straight at him, and held out his little hand to him. He gently grasped the little hand. And so, the battle done, the faithful old prelate peacefully went to his heavenly home.

Epilogue

Dr. Retief lay in his lounge chair. It seemed the bees in the Butterfly Bush were particularly loud today. He looked at his Koi, and thought. With the help of his easily sharing friend Klaas Blik he had become familiar with the early details of the twelve chosen, knowledge now supplemented by the media about the recent happening in Geneva. Half asleep he reflected on the "holy mischief" he had perpetrated upon his colleagues and, for that matter, the entire world.

By virtue of his expertise with computers, the 'hacking' into those of his ecclesiastical buddies plus the one in head office had been relatively effortless for him. It was the playing God that had been the real challenge. But, he thought, he had done alright, and hopefully the twelve would respond positively to God's loving invitation to talk over with him their frustrations, their needs, and their sorrows.

Machiavellian? Yes, probably a little bit. But he had bamboozled his friends and acquaintances with in mind only to make the God-accusers realize their criticisms were unfounded, and unfair. And that was okay, wasn't it? God wouldn't mind him having done that, would he?

Presently he smiled, and closed his eyes. Aided by the buzzing of the bees he soon was asleep, and for the next several hours The Rev. Dr. Pieter Retief slept the deep, peaceful and contented sleep of the faithful. He could, for he figured that all was well, and that all manner of thing would be well.

Richmond,
February, 2006

ISBN 141208645-0